Shasta Dam

A History of Construction, 1938-1945

Al M. Rocca, PhD

Introduction by
J. Paul Capener,
Former Area Manager of Northern California Office;
United States Bureau of Reclamation

Renown Publishing
Redding, California
www.shasta.com/renown

in cooperation with

CreateSpace

Scotts Valley, CA 95066
www.createspace.com

Author: Rocca, Al M., 1949-

Shasta Dam: A History of Construction, 1938-1945

Non-Fiction, 116 pages

1. Dams—West (U.S.)—History. 2. Irrigation—West (U.S.)—History. I Title.

ISBN: 1442149086   EAN-13: 9781442149083

First Printing: 2009

All photos are used with permission from the United States Bureau of Reclamation and the Library of Congress.

Personal and anecdotal text block material used with permission by Marion Allen (taken from *The Headtower* and *Shasta Dam and Its Builders*)

Table of Contents

Frank Crowe, Superintendent of Construction

Foreword

Shasta Dam today remains one of the world's great engineering achievements. Tourists from all over America, and many countries, continue to visit and marvel at this massive concrete monolith. Within the United States, only Grand Coulee Dam in Washington state is wider, and only Hoover and Glen Canyon Dams are taller. Set against the backdrop of majestic Mt. Shasta and beautiful Lake Shasta, Shasta Dam is truly one of America's scenic and technological wonders.

Between the placing of the first bucket of concrete on July 8, 1940 and the final bucket on December 22, 1944, 6,535,000 yards of concrete had been mixed, delivered and placed. This is enough concrete to build a 3-foot wide sidewalk around the world at the equator. All of this concrete resulted in a structure 602 feet tall, higher than the Washington Monument and three times taller than Niagara Falls. The roadway crest is 39 feet wide and extends 3500 feet, from east to west. Built like a pyramid, Shasta Dam is

883 feet thick at the base (including spillway apron). The downstream face of the dam covers 31 acres, while the area of the spillway is large enough to accommodate six football fields.

Other statistics involving the use of the world's longest conveyor belt and the production of hundreds of thousands of kilowatts add to the perception that the building of Shasta Dam was a national effort undertaken at a time when America desperately needed to believe in herself;

THE SHASTA DAM AND POWER PLANT

a time when Depression-weary families migrated thousands of miles in search of government sponsored work projects, with the hope of beginning a new life in California. The awesome amounts of time and labor spent in building Shasta Dam also point to the patriotic commitment that thousands of workers unceasingly gave throughout the hostilities of World War II. Early in the war, it was realized

6

that Shasta Dam's proposed hydroelectric capacity would be needed to power the new shipbuilding facilities being constructed in Richmond, Oakland, and Alameda. To speed completion, the Pentagon declared the Shasta project to be a AA-1 defense related project, thereby receiving priority status in the acquisition of money, materials, and labor.

As part of the overall war effort Shasta Dam took on a special meaning for residents in northern California. The government, through media propaganda, asked citizens to give their all. And give they did. At the dam site, thousands toiled through bitter winter cold, plodding to work during heavier than usual snowfalls. Workers struggled through the great flood of 1940, rescuing isolated families and moving equipment to higher ground. Every summer they sweated, as the infamous August heat waves caused temperatures to soar over 110°. All of this the workers endured with an incredibly good safety record. Ralph Lowry, top government inspector and Frank Crowe, superintendent of

construction, insisted and worked hard on keeping accidents down. Safety rules were strictly enforced and violators quickly reprimanded.

While the urgency of generating electrical power for the war effort focused attention on Shasta Dam, the main

purpose in its construction lay in the attempt to solve California's historic water problems. Shasta Dam would become the "keystone" of the Central Valley Project, the United States Bureau of Reclamation's plan to store water for domestic and irrigation use, control flooding along the Sacramento River, regulate salinity levels in the lower Sacramento Delta, improve water quality, allow for reliable river navigation levels, promote fish conservation, and supply electrical power.

For 65 years Shasta Dam has, without interruption, provided Californians with the above-mentioned benefits. Today, Shasta Dam is the "cornerstone" of California's agricultural economy and the most important component in supplying water to the continually expanding urban centers of northern California.

It is my hope to reveal in this book, both the engineering perspective, its scale and innovation, and the human drama--the life and times of ordinary Americans struggling to shake off the economic doldrums of the Great Depression and the rationing of World War II. In the course of writing this book I interviewed more than 150 former dam workers and their families. Many of them remember their association with Shasta Dam as one of the most important events in their life. Their dedication to excellence and commitment to finish the job ahead of schedule serve as a lasting testimonial to the American tradition of pulling together, working hard, and completing the task.

This book is in its second printing and some changes have occurred in terms of text updating and photos substituted. I would like to continue to thank the U.S. Bureau of Reclamation for use of the excellent photographs of the construction process.

I would like to mention a few of the many persons responsible for this publication. First and foremost, I want to express my deepest appreciation to Mr. J. Paul Capener, former Area Manager for the U.S. Bureau of Reclamation for allowing me access into the Shasta Dam archives and for writing the wonderful Introduction to this book. I also want to thank the Shasta Dam tour guides, especially Sheri Harral and Tami Corn, for sharing their expertise on the engineering aspects of construction and for describing the personal experiences of numerous dam workers.

Much of the primary source material used in this book is drawn from *The Headtower*, the newsletter published regularly during the construction years. I also wish to thank the late Marion Allen. He re-published the interesting, and popular book, *Shasta Dam and Its Builders* (originally published by Pacific Constructors Inc.) and I have drawn much from this work. It is to Allen that this book is dedicated.

Introduction

I never tire of watching Her, Shasta Dam, that is. She represents more than a monolith of strength, indeed more than a wonderment of science. At times it is as if She whispers a marvelous and wondrous story. In the silence of the late afternoon, She tells Her story as the evening shadows dance across Her face, bringing to life with the casual observer might mistake as lifeless concrete. A story of courageous people spanning centuries of time, She tells of Pythagoras, Euclid and Archimedes, who, over 2000 years ago, laid the foundations of geometry upon which, a thousand years later, mathematicians such as Newton, Leibniz, and Bernoulli would develop the tools required by engineers to convert the dreams of visionaries into the challenges of the builder.

She tells of the unleashed fury of nature that for centuries unrelentingly scoured Her canyon walls with ravaging floodwaters, sent thundering into the valley below to baptize all within its bounds, and then, as if to tantalize, would withhold the life-giving stream when needed most to quench the scorching thirst of the valley.

She tells of those who came by the thousands to unearth the very rocks which She now rests, searching for riches and power, not realizing that the very spot which

brought forth "fools' riches " would one day be the source of undreamed riches for tens of thousands willing to rise to the challenge .

She tells of the valley fields that now flourish and prosper, as they drink from her cool water sent down from behind Her impenetrable walls, of the security felt by those spared the destruction of the winter floods and of the many factories humming with power generated at Her side.

Her most cherished stories, and I sense this to be the case, as She always waits until the shadows of the evening have chased away the days last fleeting hope, are those of the modern-day pioneers who arrived at the dawn of a new day, the beginning of Her day. They came with a strong back, a clear mind and a determination of heart to literally create with their own hands that which had been created in the minds of others. They came from all over the land. They came by rail, in old hissing autos, and even on foot. These are the stories of those who gave life to the steel as they tied and bound it, whose sweat is mixed within Her concrete, who labored under the relentless heat of the day to bathe Her concrete face with cool water as She was gaining strength in Her infancy. They tended to Her every need, both day and night, day after day, month after month, year after year, until that day arrived when, with great jubilation, they joined in one loud chorus "it is finished!" Then, with feelings of both great satisfaction and the sadness of heart, the builders, the real story of Shasta, one by one left, some by rail, some in old hissing autos, and even some on foot, but all of them much greater in stature, having been a part of the creation reserved for the few. Some say their voices can even now be heard echoing through the miles of passageways carved deep within Her body.

This is their story. You'll see it within the pages of this book, in the faces captured by the photographer's camera; you will see it as their labors are transformed into immovable concrete. If you want to hear Her tell it, stop by some quiet summer day, preferably in the late afternoon, perhaps She will tell it to you as She has told it to me.

J. Paul Capener
Former, Area Manager of Northern California Office
United States Bureau of Reclamation

Chapter 1
The Central Valley Project

Ever since European colonization of California began under the Spanish in the 1700s, it became obvious that water conservation and supply ranked as the most difficult problems to overcome. Early settlement, even under the Americans, concentrated along river banks and links. A problem centered on the fact that California's Mediterranean climate brought rain in the winter, followed by an extensive dry summer. To make matters worse, most of the rain and snow fell in the distant northern portions of the state and in the Sierra Nevada Mountains; the water was largely inaccessible to population centers in the south and along the coast. The debate and discussion focused on how to capture, store, and deliver the water sources, and to what degree should government become involved.

California statehood coincided with a severe drought and the first lawmakers provided that one of the principle duties of the new position of surveyor-general included planning water developments. Droughts continued, with an especially long one in the 1863–1864 water-year. Grain crops throughout the state wilted, and state officials worried about feeding the increasing ways of newcomers. Everyone knew that irrigation could ease the problems. The tricky land-use and water-use rights stood in the way.

Lawmakers in 1864 set the stage for state involvement by authorizing the incorporation of canal companies and irrigation districts. In addition, state water planners began drawing water source diagrams to assist local and regional water districts.

In 1873, president Ulysses S. Grant ordered a team of hydrologists in the Army Engineers to serve a water sources in California's Central Valley. The team worked at identifying potential water concentrations, posing future dam sites, and projecting canal links. Numerous farmers and cattle ranchers contributed their advice. Grant reported to Congress that the Central Valley was a great untapped agricultural resource that only needed irrigation to be one of America's most productive farming regions. The next year Californian B. S. Alexander proposed an idea that was to become the basic water plan of the Central Valley Project. Alexander argued that surplus water in the northstate should be dammed and transported south using canals and aqueducts. The dams would curtail chronic flooding, generate electricity, and provide irrigation of the dry San Joaquin Valley. While his ideas appeared noteworthy, most Californians, including jurists working in the legal system, dismissed the practicality of implementing a statewide water plan. Dozens of water rights' litigation

President U. S. Grant

cases had already proven that any provocative comprehensive water plan would face substantial opposition in the California courts.

The next 40 years realized little movement by California to incorporate a statewide water system. The Army Corps of Engineers along with the Reclamation Service conducted more surveys of potential water sources and analyzed canal routes, yet organized political action did not materialize. A geographer for the United States Geological Survey, Colonel Robert B. Marshall, saw the need to have the California state legislature take the

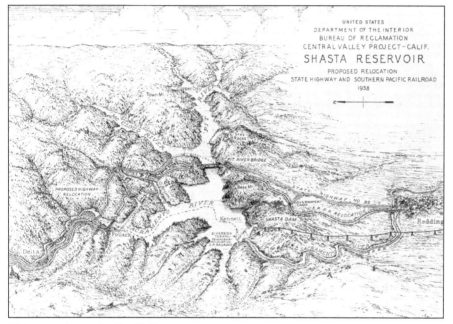

This map drawn for the U. S. Bureau of Reclamation provides a view of the proposed dam and reservoir.

lead in proposing and funding a water plan. Marshall produced his informative *Irrigation of 12 million acres in the Valley of California* in 1921, and immediately it gained statewide and national attention. He pointed to the need for a concentration of local irrigation districts/projects to be regulated by a state water commission. Marshall also proposed that a huge dam be constructed near the headwaters of the Sacramento River, taking advantage of the river's traditional heavy winter flow. From here, the storm water would be pumped south and parceled out by state water officials. The canals Marshall planed included

16

several wide prototypes, capable of barge navigation, located on both the east and west sides of the Central Valley. Publicity for Marshall's book helped gain the attention of the state legislature. A state scientific investigation of Marshall's ideas followed, but a subsequent implementation plan, the Water and Power Bill, went down to defeat as the legislature could not find the means to finance a project of that extent. All through the 1920s progressive planners put the Marshall bill on the ballot as a peoples' initiative measure. A well planned and financed opposition lead by Pacific Gas & Electric Company put out literature helping to defeat the proposal year after year.

By 1933 conditions in California, and the nation had changed. Gripped in a disastrous depression, liberals and conservatives alike understood that a comprehensive water plan would be necessary for California to recover. With much of the Midwest torn asunder by the driving "Dust Bowl," federal "New Deal" planners also knew that California played a vital role in

"Boomtown" children living in Central Valley

helping to relieve the pressure of long-term unemployment. If only water could be delivered to the Central Valley, farmers would have a chance at a productive and profitable recovery. State officials also realized the opportunity they had in securing federal dollars to fund the water project. To this end, the state legislature passed the Central Valley Project Act in 1933, authorizing a bond promise totaling $170 million. Private power companies forced the state to place the initiative on the ballot again. This time, the people supported the proposal passing it by a narrow margin of 30,000 votes out of 900,000.

Proposal proponents such as Judge Francis Carr and State Senator John McColl, both northern California residents, traveled to Washington, D.C. to convince the federal government to fund the state proposal. They knew that the government had already authorized funds for the construction of Hoover Dam, and work was already moving ahead on that project. Carr and McColl also knew that any statewide plan needed to include a huge dam somewhere in northern California. The project would generate a permanent income for the area; an area that had been in an economic depression ever since the end of World War I and the closing of the profitable copper mines and smelters. They lobbied hard and long, along with many other California water progressives, both Democrat and Republican.

Success came in 1935 when Congress passed the Rivers and Harbors Act. Some $12 million were allocated to the Central Valley Project. Subsequent legislation provided additional funding, as the project's full scope became known. The work was to begin on two new dams, one in northern California (Shasta) to harness the

Sacramento River, and one in central California (Friant) to hold back the rapid waters of the San Joaquin River. Canals, aqueducts, pumping stations, smaller dams, and electrical transmission lines would all be added later. Ambitious in design and gigantic in nature, the Central Valley Project would provide America's fastest growing state with water and energy.

As excitement grew with the federal government's decision to fund the project, questions remained as to who would actually build the major component–Shasta Dam. Using the Hoover Dam experience as a model, Congress gave the United States Bureau of Reclamation authority to oversee dam construction. The Bureau quickly placed the

Henry Kaiser

Shasta Dam project under the New Deal funding agency of the Public Works Administration (PWA) thereby ensuring an ongoing funding commitment from Congress. Additionally, the Bureau decided to "bid out" dam construction to private companies as had been done on Hoover Dam. There, a construction conglomerate known as Six Companies, led by Henry Kaiser, was successfully completing that dam. Since no single construction company would have the necessary manpower and resources to build a giant dam, the idea of combining construction companies into incorporated "joint ventures" became a practical, and therefore, a popular solution.

Pacific Constructors Incorporated (PCI) came into existence in 1937 when William A. Johnson, a leading southern California industrialist, successfully convinced other construction owners to form a joint venture and bid on federal dam projects. Johnson brought in Steve Griffith, L. E. Dixon, Clyde Wood, Floyd Shofner, and the D. W. Thurston, all experienced in completing heavy construction jobs. Their first bid on Grand Coulee Dam in the state of Washington showed their inexperience in bidding for a large dam project. They overbid by $8 million, an embarrassingly high amount. Yet, from this miscalculation, the young construction consortium gained experience in bidding and they used this experience to help them on the subsequent Shasta Dam bid.

In preparing to bid on the Shasta Dam job, the leadership team of Pacific Constructors decided to bring in additional construction companies, the best in the nation. To this end, the Arundel Corporation, W. E. Callahan Construction Company, Gunther & Shirley Company, and the Foley Brothers Incorporated, all accepted the invitation to join the bid on Shasta Dam. Most of the newcomers were anxious to acquire the job, but announced that they wanted to bid a "good safe figure" assuring them a profit. It was understood that trying to calculate all the unseen expenses on a job the size of Shasta was the most difficult, and extended delays could provoke financial reprisals from the federal government and destroy profits.

Bids for construction of Shasta Dam were called for by the U.S. Bureau of Reclamation beginning April 1, 1938. A bid bond or certified check for $2 million was required with each bid and a performance bond of $5 million along with a payment bond of an additional $2.5 million was specified at the time the job was awarded. Pacific

---

Construction Bids

The U.S. Bureau of Reclamation, by 1937, had a long history of bidding out its biggest irrigation construction projects. Bidding for large projects, such as dams, could be disastrous if the private companies did not take every possible contingency into consideration—including: materials, transportation, labor, weather, housing for workers, and engineering challenges. No one was better at bidding for dams than Frank T. Crowe, who had more experience bidding and building dams than anyone else in the country. His low bid for the Hoover Dam project, provided huge profits for his sponsoring employer—Six Companies Inc.

Constructors collected $3 million in capital that was used by a combination of surety companies to provide the necessary bonds.

With the bonds secured, dozens of engineers from most of the associated companies of Pacific Constructors journeyed to the expected dam site, some ten miles north of Redding on the Sacramento River, and began to put together bids. Among these engineers Ray Whinnery, Harvey Slocum, and L. E. Dixon took the lead. They collaborated on engineering techniques and cost estimates. All figures were checked and rechecked with the understanding that only a calculated low bid would wrest the job bid away from their sure and previous competitor, Six Companies. It is interesting to note that the bidding engineers needed to work through every phase of the operation, from surveying and excavation to concrete placing and finishing. Since no existing support services were located near the building site, estimators planned for the building of an entire community: homes, dormitories, a mess hall, a recreation hall, a fire station, sheds, workshops, a hospital, and an administrative center.

The most significant factor to be considered in estimating the Shasta Dam job focused on the method of concrete delivery. What would be the most cost effective manner in which to place the freshly mixed concrete into the correct form? Traditionally, concrete placing on large construction jobs had seen a variety of techniques used including movable troughs, trolley car dumpsters even animal pull carts. By 1930, most methods utilized an arrangement of cables that were anchored to one or more

Workers leave their shift after raising a frame for a new workshop at the Shasta Dam site.

PCI bid for Shasta Dam

The final bid price was arrived at in an amusing way. Carl Swenson [Foley Brothers, Inc.] was on the low side and was one of the leaders of that faction, arguing their cause long and forcefully. His wise old father, O. W. Swenson, had attended all the meetings and made a study of the estimates in his own quiet way. When price discussions got under way (and before anyone got down to naming a figure), he did a little figuring on the back of an envelope and on a card he wrote his idea of a price for the job. He handed the card to Bill [William] Johnson and left the meeting. Bill proved to be among the highs and as usual took a leading part in the discussion. After the highs and lows had argued back and forth for a couple of hours the highs agreed among themselves to come down to $36,000,000. Bill, knowing that the figure on the card was about $35,990,000, said to Carl, "We will compromise with your father's figure," and pulled out the card. Carl was reluctant to give in, but stated very graciously that he would defer to his father's judgment and the others then fell in line, and the old gentleman's figure was agreed upon. When Joe Hogan accepted, he remarked that he would accept any price the group agreed on but if we bid over $34,000,000 we were just wasting our time. As it turned out, after the months of toil and effort estimating and figuring, it was the more or less psychic bid of a contractor of the old school that finally set the price for Shasta Dam.

--J. C. Maguire

trestle mastheads. The buckets of concrete moved along the cableway and were dumped into the appropriate form. The real problem was to decide on the most efficient cable system. For this PCI looked at previous cable systems used at Hoover and Parker dams.

Other parameters needed to be considered. Even though the New Deal legislation cranked out federal funds at a never before seen pace and optimism ran high--at least among most Democrats, the economic future remained uncertain. How do you calculate for inflation on a construction job that is planned to hire thousands of workers and extend six years in duration? Will Japanese aggression in China lead to war with the U.S. and will we be dragged into the deepening European crisis? Wages set by the federal government could be changed at any time. If the Depression economics dictate, would Congress raise the minimum wage in response to popular demand? PCI officials also worried about the numerous subcontractors. Could they be counted on to go the duration of the project, supplying materials and labor as needed and at the efficiency level expected?

Meeting at the Biltmore Hotel in Los Angeles, PCI partners considered the above questions and negotiated a bid. Ironically, most of the late joiners, Eastern companies like Arundel argued for a low bid of $34 million, while most of the original core of PCI companies stated that it would take $36 or $37 million to complete the dam. J. C. Maguire, Secretary for PCI, remembered how the final bid was arrived at. The story is told in the side bar at left.

At 10:00 am on June 1, 1938, the bids were opened in Sacramento, California. As expected only two bids surfaced, that of PCI and their arch rivals, the overconfident Six Companies (by this time they had reorganized and renamed themselves the Shasta Construction Company). The opposing bids proved to be amazingly close, PCI offered to do the job for $35,939,450 while Shasta Construction followed with $36,202,357. PCI had won! Finally, they had succeeded in acquiring a major federal dam contract. After a brief, but intensive effort on the part of Shasta Construction to invalidate the PCI bid, the Bureau of Reclamation ruled that the submitted bids were to be honored and that PCI would be given the contract.

Meanwhile, PCI reorganized, added new member companies, formed committees to handle different phases of the job, and searched for a General Superintendent. They needed an experienced dam construction engineer, someone who could handle the intricate and oftentimes frustrating operational relationship between the U. S. Bureau of Reclamation inspectors, contracting construction company managers and supervisors, and the thousands of newly hired laborers. To PCI's good fortune, America's top dam builder, Frank T. Crowe, was just finishing his work on Parker Dam, and he applied and secured the position. Crowe had already been nationally recognized for his masterful handling of the tough Hoover Dam project. His reputation as a tough, yet fair, and rewarding supervisor had earned him the loyalty of hundreds of "construction stiffs" who looked to Crowe for future job opportunities. PCI knew that by hiring Crowe,

Frank Crowe (left) looking over the Shasta Dam site with engineers from the U.S. Bureau of Reclamation.

you were also hiring an already tested and proven dam construction crew--the best in the nation, or the world, for that matter.

The word went out nationwide, and Crowe's loyal band of dam builders migrated to Shasta County throughout the summer of 1938. Typical of these devoted dam builders was Lloyd Hill. Hill began his dam building experience as a young man on the San Gabriel Canyon Dams. Clearing rock debris from tunnel excavations, the impressionable Hill, learned just how demanding and dangerous dam work could be. By 1932, he moved on to Morris Dam, which supplied water to Pasadena. He worked his way up the construction ladder from concrete placing "stiff" to the carpenter shop. One day while working on an abutment slope, a bucket of cobbles just ahead of him broke loose from the cableway. Hill ran frantically, successfully dodging the oncoming missiles. Once while he was erecting new walls in the cement holding bin, a fellow worker unaware of Hill's presence, accidentally turned on a blower motor, covering Hill with cement dust in seconds. Thinking quickly, Hill scrambled to where he knew the ladder was located. Within seconds, nearby workers hearing Hill call out for help pulled him out of the swirling bin. Hill met Frank Crowe when he joined the crew at Parker Dam. He appreciated the new job opportunities that Crowe offered hard-working men. After proving himself with work on the draft tubes, Hill helped place concrete on the powerhouse. Finally, he moved to the dam, where he set the finished handrails. As he completed the finishing work on Parker Dam, Hill was approached and asked if he would be

Two of Crowe's dam workers preparing explosives during the excavation phase of construction.

24

interested in working on Shasta Dam. He remained in Pasadena for a time, where he completed his schooling and married. Upon arriving at the Shasta site in 1938, Hill was told that he would need to wait several months before he could be hired. He found work on Grand Coulee Dam in Washington during this interim period. Immediately upon his return to the Shasta area in 1939 Hill was hired to help erect the Pit River Bridge. As day foreman, he worked on the west abutment and the support piers. As he was completing this work, he received notice from Charlie Silva, a foreman at Shasta Dam, to work on the powerhouse. Eventually, Hill remained on the job after brief work stints at the Kaiser Magnesium Plant in the Bay Area. Returning to Shasta Dam, he worked a number of jobs, finally helping to tear down the gravel plant in Redding. Along with these veteran dam builders, came hundreds of other men and their families, hoping to join the PCI team.

The United States Bureau of Reclamation, given the authority to oversee the work of PCI, selected durable and proven Ralph Lowry as Chief Engineer. Lowry would work closely with Frank Crowe, Superintendent of PCI, and together they made most of the important decisions concerning construction.

Ralph Lowry, Chief Engineer

Chapter 2
1936-38

The United States Bureau of Reclamation sent B. D. Glaha, an excellent and experienced government photographer, to the Shasta Dam area as early as May of 1936. His charge included a photo reconnaissance of the dam site, both upstream and downstream photos. Sequentially, Glaha worked his way up the Pit, McCloud, and Sacramento River arms clicking shots of abandoned mining towns like Kennett and Coram. He paid particular attention to photographing sections of the Southern Pacific tracks through that area. Miles of these railroad tracks would be relocated to higher elevations, above the planned reservoir water levels. Glaha photographed the McCloud fish hatchery at Baird, the highway bridge over the Pit River, the large bridge at Pollock, and the confluence of the Pit and McCloud Rivers; he even caught a frustrated prospector panning for gold in the cool water of the Sacramento River.

Most of his photos reveal the rough mountainous topography that is typical of the entire area north of Redding. This region is heavily forested with Digger Pine, Manzanita brush, oaks, and assorted conifers. Mountain streams cut their way through miles of treacherous steep canyons, making communication and transportation difficult. Highway 99, the main north/south connection crossed numerous small bridges and Glaha wanted to photograph all bridges that might be affected by the future reservoir or that would be involved in the transportation system keyed to bring in materials to the dam site. Sharp turns in Highway 99 were noted, as they could prevent very large trucks and trailers from carrying massive steel girders and huge electric and hydraulic machinery. Glaha, stationed in Redding, took pictures around Redding, recording the already existing water projects, such as the Anderson-Cottonwood Diversion Works and intake canal.

By June of 1936, Glaha moved quickly day after day throughout the proposed dam site area. He was shocked to see the extensive former copper mines and smelters. These small isolated industrial communities lay abandoned at Bully Hill, Copper City, Heroult, Matheson, Keswick, Coram, and Kennett. Many of the buildings remained standing, ghosts of the past, including hotels, homes, and saloons. One of the most

Old buildings in the town of Kennett.

spectacular sights of Glaha's visits to these smelter and mining sites was the prevalence of barren hillsides. The surrounding hills, in all directions revealed an eerie

27

defoliation. The denuding of vegetation, caused by the highly toxic copper smelting fumes, gave the appearance of a stark and ruined landscape. Near all of these sites Glaha found recent attempts at gold mining. Extensive large-scale dredging had occurred near Newtown, just north of Redding. Local residents told him that heavy machinery had been brought in the year before and that the operation had dredged for a full year. Little gold had been found. Glaha paid particular attention to the gigantic dredging scene around Clear Creek, south of Redding. When he arrived on the scene, a flurry of activity was observed. Dredging rigs were being erected all along Clear Creek. Millions of cubic yards of dredger waste, basically gravel, lined the banks of Clear Creek for miles. Glaha estimated one very large deposit, an 18 million cubic yards of gravel covering 420 acres, stretching almost two miles. Of course, these deposits could be used for the enormous amounts of concrete that would have to be mixed at the dam site. But, Glaha remarked that this deposit was 19 miles from the dam site, and while the material appeared to be limited to a maximum size of nine inches there seemed to be a deficiency of sand and small gravel.

Glaha developed his pictures and reported his findings to the Bureau of Reclamation in July of 1936. While plans moved ahead for the building of Shasta Dam in 1937, the Bureau sent Glaha back to the area to take additional photographs. He arrived in May to take photos far to the north at the Upper Table Mountain dam site, part of the original Kennett Division. Glaha remained on the scene at the Kennett dam site to witness, and photograph, an official Congressional visit by members of the Interior Department Subcommittee (House of Representatives). Arriving by train on September 5, the group posed for ceremonial picture taking. The group was accompanied by Walker R. Young, Construction Engineer for the Bureau of Reclamation and John B. McColl, California State Senator and longtime proponent of the Central Valley Project. One week later, United States Bureau of Reclamation Commissioner, John C. Page, was on hand to dedicate the initiation of the project. At this time, he officially renamed the dam, Shasta. His multi-paged remarks centered on the benefits expected from the completion of Shasta Dam and the resulting Central Valley Project. After his comments were over, local politicians, such as Redding Mayor August Gronwoldt, described how the Shasta Dam project would provide a "shot in the arm" to the dragging northstate economy.

Almost immediately, government survey crews laid out Kennett Camp (later renamed Toyon), headquarters and home to hundreds of Bureau inspectors, engineers, and other personnel. By late January of 1938, construction was well under way. The main administrative building, dormitories, warehouses, a testing laboratory, garage and fire station, and dozens of small homes neared completion. The government

Dormitories at the Government Camp (Toyon)

wanted to show the benefits of "New Deal" program dollars, and they made the construction live up to exacting building standards. In fact, when completed, Toyon shined as a government model community. Full services, including running water, sewer, and electricity were available from the start. Home design and construction gave the appearance of a well-ordered, inviting environment. Toyon residents such as George Van Eaton remarked that "everyone" wanted to live there. It helped exude a feeling of stability in the economic chaos of the Depression. But,

Cascade Theater in Redding. 1938.

everyone could not live there. Housing was limited in Toyon, and a waiting list quickly developed.

The housing shortage reached critical levels by mid-1938 as hundreds of unemployed men converged on Redding and the dam site area. Quick thinking and profit-minded entrepreneurs from Redding, Sacramento, and the Bay Area purchased land around the newly cut in access road from Highway 99. The road, first named Grand Coulee Boulevard, was renamed Shasta Dam Boulevard; it soon became dotted with small businesses and homes. Two of the first establishments to open their doors to thirsty clients were The Silver Dollar and The Mint Pool Hall. By June, Shasta Dam Boulevard's dusty dirt surface carried considerable traffic to and from the dam site to the new growing communities nearby. Soon three community centers rose: Summit City, at the intersection of Shasta Dam Boulevard and the Kennett/Buckeye Road; Project City, at the intersection of Highway 99 and Shasta Dam Boulevard; and Central Valley, strung out for two miles on Shasta Dam

30

Boulevard between Summit City and Project City. Collectively, they became known as Boomtown.

As the weather turned from warm to hot in July and August of 1938, work began on re-routing the Southern Pacific tracks that would be impacted by dam construction or covered later with the rising waters from Shasta Lake. Down at the dam site, crews started drilling a railroad by-pass tunnel that would later double as a Sacramento River diversion tunnel. Working in thin short sleeved shirts and sporting protective shell hard hats, workers sweated to excavate into the hillside. As work progressed heavy timber was placed to support the ever-deepening tunnel. Meanwhile, men in bulldozers struggled to clear out a road to the right (east) abutment. Steep slopes made work dangerous as well as difficult. By September, crews cleared the future sites of the

The railroad by-pass tunnel later served as the river diversion tunnel. The tunnel extended over 1800 feet and was 30 feet wide. Workers used a re-usable concrete lining form. The form was moved progressively down the tunnel for final concrete placement.

hospital, and administrative offices. Also, a temporary truck bridge was built downstream from the dam site. This would afford access to the right (west) abutment. On September 21, excited men began using power shovels and trucks to excavate for the foundation of the dam on the east abutment. Though the rocky clay soil proved difficult to penetrate, work progressed at a good pace. The combination of heavy equipment and individual manual labor working alongside

31

each other was amazing. Huge digging shovels scooped up material that had been broken-up by men working hydraulic jackhammers.

It was realized that Toyon, some three miles distant, and Boomtown, two miles further, could help provide services and housing. Yet, it had been a tradition in U. S. dam building history to construct a company town at the work site. Pacific Constructors and their new Superintendent of Construction, Frank T. Crowe, realized that a substantial community would need to be built at the dam site. Thus was born Shasta Dam Village. Almost self-contained, it boasted a huge dormitory, mess hall, recreation room, dry-goods store, and single-family homes.

Almost daily through September, scores of new families arrived in the Boomtown area; the men were

Mess Hall at Shasta Dam Village

hoping for quick employment on the dam. Newly arrived residents settled in numerous squatter camps along the Sacramento River (downstream, all the way to Redding), and near Shasta Dam Boulevard. Glaha, official Bureau photographer, visited these families and recorded visually their plight. Many had only simple tent and tarp affairs for shelter. Others lived in trailers, or crude lean-to shelters built from scrap lumber. Many single men lived in their automobiles. While the

32

economic situation for these job hopefuls was bleak, they counted on Pacific Constructors to begin mass hiring once the main concrete work began. In the American spirit of cooperation, the Bureau, PCI, Shasta County Office of Education, and numerous Boomtown residents pitched in to erect a school house for children of dam workers. The Bureau supplied the land-adjacent to Toyon, PCI provided the materials. PCI workers and unemployed men raised the long rectangular structure in September and October.

Matt Rumboltz, Toyon's first principal, and three teachers planned to open the school on October 3. Advanced sign ups totaled 125 prospective students. When the school doors opened on October 10, children stormed the not-yet-finished schoolhouse. Eleven days later the student population climbed to 213 and by the end of the month 256 students had enrolled.

Toyon School

With the word out that a new school had opened, the student population steadily climbed to over 350 by the end of the year, and, peaked at 400 in January of 1939, making it one of the largest rural schools in the nation. By this time, Rumboltz had been forced to expand his staff to ten full-time teachers, and two new rooms were hastily built. Students literally began coming "out of the windows." Individual class sizes ranged from a low of 36 to an unbelievable 73 students in one first grade class! Even Rumboltz's office was converted into classroom space. The principal had to conduct his business in the hallway or outside under a tree.

With construction activity in full-swing the Bureau decided to invite Secretary of the Interior Harold L. Ickes and others to come to the Shasta site and speak about the importance of Shasta Dam on the people and economy of California. The ceremony was broadcast to most of California and it helped set off another influx of job-seeking men. Ickes was given a tour of the dam site and Toyon. He saw young Civilian Conservation Corps (CCC) employees grading driveways and landscaping the dorms. Bureau chief Lowry and PCI

Drillers busy setting blasting holes

Superintendent Crowe assured Ickes that everything was moving along on schedule, and that sufficient manpower would be available.

Late October through December realized a rapid expansion in hiring as more manpower was needed. Finishing work continued on Shasta Dam Village, as warehouses, electrical and mechanical shops, single-family homes, were all completed. Excavation began on the west abutment and continued on the east side. Groups of wagon-mounted drilling rigs operated continuously on the river

34

diversion channel and the lower abutments on both sides of the river. Designed to be operated by two men the wagon drills proved effective if properly handled. One had to be watchful and careful of the powerful pulsating steel drill. The drills could be rotated to operate in the horizontal position thereby drilling horizontal blasting holes. Initial power for the hydraulic drills came from a large eight-unit compressor house. The plant could put out 11,000 cubic feet of air per minute. They also brought down the heavy duty power shovels to the rivers' edge to remove the drilled debris.

About this time, an extensive investigation of sand and gravel deposits was taking place. A large open-air warehouse was built to house the gravel samples. Crews were sent to Clear Creek, Oroville, Cherokee, Kutras Tract in Redding, and other sites around a 30 mile radius. After careful consideration the Kutras Tract led the opposing sites; it had the quality and quantity needed to build a dam the size of Shasta. Soon an innovative and interesting method would be developed to transport the

Excavating the lower abutment

aggregate the ten miles to the dam site. Meanwhile,

construction crews installed drainage culverts, erected a railroad bridge, and built a huge water tank on the east abutment; it would supply water to the contractor's camp. Most of the heavy equipment remained engaged in digging out the hillsides of the east and west slopes. The 48-B and the 120-B Power Shovels proved to be the workhorse of these early stages of abutment excavation. A fleet of 25-cubic yard capacity dump trucks hauled the excavated debris material to dump sites upstream. Day and night the crews worked, through increasingly cooler weather.

The excavation and terracing of the abutments focused the attention of most visitors to the site. Everyday the scene changed. From the top of the east slope, crowds could watch the dramatic blasting of each abutment. Then the big shovels and dump trucks would move in removing blasted material. Some of the fill was used to terrace each slope to the exact specifications necessary. The fill needed to be tamped effectively, and this was done with heavy tractors and a "sheep's foot" tamper. Back and forth the tractors crawled compacting the debris while engineers measured the levels and monitored the quality of the fill. As Christmas 1938 drew near, work continued. The weather remained clear, yet cold. A "sea wall" for the river diversion was erected. This cement structure would confine the redirected Sacramento River

Blasting on the west abutment

water once diversion became necessary. At this time, workers laid out a gigantic warehouse near the railroad tracks. It would be here that immense steel girders, railings, tubing, and other metal construction parts would be stored.

On December 22, 1938, Byron H. Eich, a CCC official and Lowry inspected the reservoir clearing progress. Eich watched as his 18 to 25-year old cadets struggled to chop down pines and oaks, rip out manzanita brush and

Young CCC workers cutting down trees in the reservoir area

poison oak. Run like a paramilitary outfit, the CCC paid $30 a month to the young men, who had to send most of the money home to their parents. Living in barracks-like quarters, the CCC enrollees started the day at sunrise, worked hard till noon, ate a hearty lunch, then continued clearing until 5:00 pm. The youthful workers proved capable, as the brush clearing operation finished ahead of schedule and with few accidents. Shasta County had, at its peak in 1939, eleven CCC camps working on Bureau projects--a national record.

As 1938 came to a close, much had been accomplished. No less than five new communities had sprung up where previously nothing had existed. An estimated population of 3,000 to 5,000 people inhabited the area. The rerouting of the Southern Pacific railroad proceeded and the river diversion sea wall stood ready to divert the Sacramento River. Also, incredible amounts of

River diversion seawall

earth had been removed from the east and west slopes and the foundation channels deepened. Workers had constructed bridges that connected the work on both sides of the river, and they graded roads connecting the dam site with the outside world. The eyes of the nation were focusing on the area as continuing news of construction progress spread rapidly, and more and more job-hungry men migrated to the area.

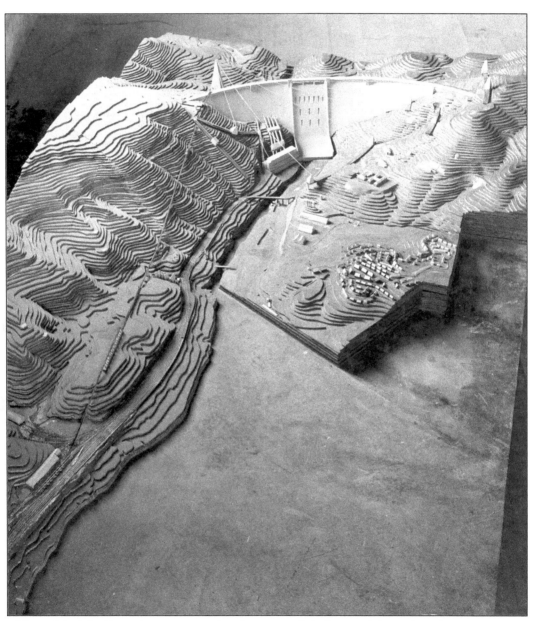

This model of the Shasta Dam construction site was made before work began by John Crowe, nephew to Frank Crowe. John, himself an engineer, wanted to layout the cableway system to scale, along with Shasta Dam Village (contractor's camp), warehouses, workshops and other buildings.

Much of the early work around the Shasta Dam site involved using bulldozers to cut in roads to the river.

Chapter 3
1939

As 1939 opened, workers returned from New Year Day celebrations feeling fortunate to have a job and eager to continue excavating the east and west abutments, digging the diversion channel along the Sacramento River, and tunneling the railroad by-pass. Every day unemployed men gathered anxiously around the hiring shack at the dam site looking for posted openings and hoping that their skill specialty would be needed. On one occasion a desperate job-seeker told a PCI foreman that he had a friend who had welding experience on Parker Dam. The foreman asked for the name of the friend, and the job-hopeful replied, "I am that man!" He was hired on the spot. The easiest way to get hired on the dam project was to let a friend who already was employed help you. Friends would talk to a foreman and managers and by informal talk a job offer would be made. Everyone understood that you had to prove yourself every day. No wimps allowed. All men reported to their work shift on time, worked hard, obeyed their supervisors,

and followed the safety rules to the letter. Superintendent Frank Crowe insisted on strict safety compliance; he did not want negative publicity about pushing work ahead at the expense of his men's safety. Crowe had seen large numbers of injuries and dozens of fatalities on the dangerous Hoover Dam project and he (and the Bureau) did not want a repeat at Shasta.

All phases of the work on Shasta Dam proved dangerous. However, in these initial stages of massive excavation, the danger factor increased with the use of high explosives employed to blast out the east and west abutments. The railroad by-pass tunnel also loomed as a potential hazard; weak structural zones and subsequent cave-ins in the cutout could be encountered at any time. Nonetheless, work pressed on. During January of 1939 workers dug deeper and deeper into the east abutment cutting an opening for the core wall--the side foundation of the dam itself. Powerful high-wattage night lights installed on both abutments kept work going throughout the night. The huge five-yard capacity buckets of the Bucyrus Erie electric shovels scooped blasted debris and poured the material into awaiting dump trucks, to be deposited where needed around the dam site. Day after day this routine continued.

Work proceeded around the clock by using powerful lights.

Down in the railroad bypass tunnel crews struggled, working from both the north and south ends. In the dark, damp reaches of the tunnelhead men labored to drill the tunnel facing, power shovel the debris onto awaiting "muck carts" and transport the "muck" via a rail track to larger dump trucks outside the tunnel. At a proposed length of 1820 feet, an excavated height of 32 feet, and a width of 30 feet, tunnel diggers realized the immensity of their part of the project. The tunneling process involved raw excavation, initial timbering support followed by steel ribbing, placement of a reusable concrete lining form, interior cross-bracing, concrete pumping into the form, and final concrete tamping and finishing. The horseshoe-shaped form would then be moved down to the next section of braced tunnel and the concrete process would repeat. The distance from the form to the excavated edge of rock averaged two feet and this area was filled with an extensive network of reinforcing rods before concrete was pumped in. In a situation similar to America's first transcontinental railroad building race between the Union Pacific and the Central Pacific railroads, tunneling crews raced from both ends to excavate the furthest. No doubt off-duty diggers discussed their progress and wagered on the breakthrough date.

Preparing the diversion tunnel for final concrete lining

In February, scores of CCC youths continued their landscaping duties at the government camp of Toyon. Of primary importance was the administrative center. Just off Shasta Dam Boulevard, dam workers, local residents, and visiting dignitaries saw it first; and the government wanted to create a positive environment. Soon manicured lawns bordered by decorative boulders adorned the administrative center and many of the homes. To keep the appearance beautiful and orderly, individual home sites were carefully monitored. Residents were prohibited from altering the

Toyon homes

structure or radically changing the landscaping without permission from Ralph Lowry. Few complained about this lack of individual rights, in fact, most thought it was necessary and good; they felt fortunate to be living there. In the single men's dormitory, workers had a raucous good time. After finishing the daytime work shift, Toyon men ate dinner in the mess hall at Shasta Dam Village or in one of the eateries in the nearby boomtowns; there were no dining facilities at Toyon. Since Toyon was a government installation, liquor could not be served; again workers would pile into friends' cars and off they would go to Boomtown. There they could relax drinking beer, playing pool or cards, and "shooting the bull." And "shoot the bull" they did. One story led to another, as the hours passed by. Most stories centered around a worker's previous experiences working on other dam projects. Hoover Dam veterans loved to talk about the terrific danger involved in

The Workers

Many of the Shasta Dam workers knew each other from previous experiences working on earlier dams such as Deadwood, Hoover and Parker Dams. Each member of a work crew developed strong bonds of respect and friendship, both on and off the job. The relationships formed lasted for many years after their work on Shasta Dam.

their work on Black Canyon. Fort Peck Dam builders spoke about the unique problems of building an earth-filled dam. All this drinking and bravado sometimes led to impromptu physical outbursts regarding the accuracy of someone's statement. More often than this, social mixing such as this produced a strong bond of friendship and camaraderie that lasted on the job as well as off.

On March 5, drillers from the southern side broke though to the drillers coming the other way. Quickly, the small hole was enlarged big enough to fit a man, and after laying down a 2x12-inch board for support, a grimy, dirt-covered driller crawled through the orifice and greeted his companions on the north side. Preparations followed to cut open the last section and prepare for the final concrete placing. One job down! Celebrations lasted for at least two days.

Members of the American Society of Civil Engineers visited the dam site in March. Lowry had invited them to see the progress on the dam and give them a close-up view of some of the innovative engineering techniques that accompany each new job. The group was particularly impressed with the completed diversion tunnel and the

A shift foreman reads the status chart to see where he will work. Blocks with colored circles indicate areas that are currently active in preparing for concrete placing.

excellent planning that Lowry and Crowe had worked out. The engineers saw well coordinated batteries of wagon drills moving ahead with abutment excavation--drilling blasting holes at night and chipping away at critical rock fracture points in the daytime. The visitors knew that on a job the size of Shasta every aspect of the engineering must be well managed. Each phase complements and is depended on the other phases. Crew foremen reported to Bureau team inspectors who in turn checked in with PCI shift foremen. The shift foremen consulted with Lowry and Crowe constantly, looking back to review progress, correct mistakes, and anticipate upcoming problems.

April of 1939 saw attention return to the main excavation on the slope abutments. Large-scale blasting rocked the west abutment on April 12. More and more newly hired men joined the wagon-drill teams as they carved deeper into the hillside. Now agile workers scaling the steep walls of the uppermost portion of the west abutment hand dug blasting holes. Others, dangling from security ropes fastened to anchor posts chipped, dug, and shoveled rock debris. At an elevation of over 900 feet, the view was spectacular, yet frightening.

Amid all this activity hundreds of new visitors converged on the dam site, many to see the blasting. Politicians from the California State Legislature and officials from the Central Valley Project Association checked in regularly during this time period. On May 13, 1939, more than 275 visitors appeared.

Drillers working the
abutment walls

Officials of Pacific Constructors Inc. including Frank Crowe, Clyde Woods, S. M. Griffith, and W. A. Johnson entertained most of this party with a special luncheon at the company mess hall. These visitors were able to see new work beginning on the spillway section. They watched as tons of dirt and rock were cleared away. Some of the earth was taken to a newly constructed testing laboratory where tests provided information on where best to use the material. The control laboratory boasted an elaborate chemistry

The "Woody" was used to collect aggregate samples from various test sites all around Shasta County.

bench, an automatic screening hopper and special storage racks. Here concrete samples were dried, stressed and tested. All phases of concrete mixing, pouring, placing and hardening occurred in the laboratory in miniature scale. These same visitors watched as excavation began for the footings of the headtower. Huge 18-B cranes assisted in this task. In preparation for all the concrete placing that would soon be occurring a new search began for additional sources of aggregate. To this end a special mobile aggregate testing unit, a converted woody station wagon, roamed the area in search of aggregate samples.

On another occasion, June 3rd, over 100 CCC enrollees from camp BR-78, Orland Project, accompanied by project officials toured the Shasta site. Sporting brown army-like uniforms, boots, ties and African safari hats, these

48

young men observed the advance stages of excavation. They also were able to see the now completed buildings and landscaping at the Government Camp (Toyon). With lawns in, curtains in the windows, cars parked on the streets, and patio furniture in the back yard, the visitors saw a clean, park-like well maintained environment.

By June 7, blasting activity increased as PCI planners moved forward with the excavation of the spillway channel. Tons of dynamite exploded all during the following week and thousands of tons of debris were hauled away as dump trucks worked day and night. Now, coordination of all the blasting, hauling, drilling, and concrete placing became paramount. In a relatively compact area the safety of hundreds of workers' lives depended on knowing what each work crew was doing. For example, during blasting activity, tunnel workers cleared the area, trucks stopped, and drill crews took a break. Some of the crews moved from the immediate dam site canyon to the east abutment roadway. Here a preliminary application of road pavement began. This would be particularly helpful once the winter rains began in October. Already several truck accidents had occurred due to loose dirt roadway sections.

Excavation nearly complete on the east abutment

49

Through the long hot summer months of June, July, and August, off-duty dam workers, and teenagers formed summer softball leagues. The Bureau fielded a team of 16 players. They competed with local leagues from Shasta Dam Village and the Boomtowns. For added competition teams from nearby Redding and Anderson played on a regular basis. By August of 1939, the competition was so keen that numerous wagers occurred and a championship tournament completed the competition in August. Despite the repressive summer heat the competition was surprisingly high. Events such as this helped to foster a positive social environment and keep morale high. Makeshift ballparks sprang up on both abutments, across from Toyon, and several locations in the Boomtown area.

Day care children at Toyon Community Center

Meanwhile, massive amounts of fill were dumped on the west abutment lower section to form the base for the penstock slide slope. The penstocks, once installed, would carry the water to the hydroelectric turbines. At the same time the area was excavated for the powerhouse, which would be located several hundred feet downstream.

All through the month of September, activity increased away from the dam site. The aggregate plant at Kutras Tract (Redding) needed to be developed. It would be from here that excavated aggregate, of varying size and quality, would be sorted, and delivered to the mixing plant at Shasta Dam, some 10 miles to the North. An elaborate plan using a three-foot wide conveyor belt had been conceived as the most efficient way to transport the millions of tons of gravel. The foundation for the aggregate sorting

World's longest conveyor belt

plant began at a point on the Kutras Tract where the Sacramento River takes a sharp turn south. Working at the other end crews began laying the foundation for the concrete mixing plant and for the aggregate handling and storage area. Both of these facilities, located on the west side of the river and downstream from the site, would take weeks to complete. Supplemental aggregate collection sites, at Cottonwood and Anderson, California, would help supply additional mixing material. While construction of the aggregate site at Kutras moved ahead rapidly, PCI officials went to San Jose, California and there concluded a contract with Permanente Cement Company to supply the tons of needed cement. All through the summer months the Permanente facilities expanded, including additional storage silos, blending silos, a laboratory cement crusher, a new kiln, and an extensive conveyor belt operation.

October saw the beginning of work on the foundation construction and the initial stages of erecting the steel girders for the giant cableway headtower. It would be from

The headtower

this headtower that a series of cables would deliver precisely mixed concrete to specific points on the dam. For months to come, October 1939 to June of 1940, the headtower would grow like a giant erector set-- one girder at a time. Planned to be over 465 feet tall, the foundation girders extended an additional 102 feet below the surface. As the headtower grew daily so did the tailtowers, the anchor supports for the other end of the cable system. These tailtowers erected at strategic points on the downstream side of the dam, would be moveable, sliding back and forth on tracks and allowing for the exact placement of concrete.

Scores of workers now were hired to place the concrete and wood supports for the aggregate conveyor belt. Built in a series of flights, each extending for hundreds of feet, the belt would be powered uphill by electric motors. These motors would be further charged by generators that operated when the belts ran downhill. Once in operation, the belt would run continuously for five years.

As 1939 came to a close, work on the lower portions of the dam site halted with an unexpected flooding of the Sacramento River. Crews working on the powerhouse excavation and diversion channel could not continue with safety. They were assigned other jobs at higher elevations.

Headtower Construction

The massive headtower claimed the attention of most visitors to the dam site. In this photo you can see the west abutment being excavated. Note the sign next to the worker. It warms visitors not to "cross the fence."

The flooding quickly subsided, but the brief deluge revealed to PCI officials and government inspectors that proper planning for future flooding would be critical. And so it would be with the 1940 flood.

Chapter 4
1940

On January 2, 1940, construction "stiffs" remained busy in Redding as they prepared the aggregate storage units, sorting rooms, and readied the conveyor belt. That same morning, down at the dam site, a long freight train puffed and chugged its way through the work area. By now, many trains had come through the temporary railroad tunnel by-pass. It must have been quite a sight for train engineers and passengers to see, first-hand and up close, the large scale reality of the Shasta Dam project. From the train, it would have appeared that the Sacramento River had swelled with recent rains, as the swiftly running and rising water loomed only 20 feet below. Over at the Kutras Tract, concern mounted also as rapidly moving waters threatened the installation schedule of the aggregate plant. Upstream creeks such as Little Cow Creek, Cedar Creek, and the Pit River crested; beautiful Burney Falls dumped surplus water through cracks on both sides of the main spillway. Mount

Shasta, in the distance stood majestically covered, with snow levels dropping dramatically.

By mid-January the rain had stopped and the ground began to dry out. Crowe and Lowry drove their crews to make up lost time, and work proceeded on erecting ten large cement silos near the main aggregate storage unit at the dam site. Of course, attention remained fixed on building the main headtower. Plans called for installing the giant headtower girders in layers, or panels. The bottom panel, the longest, stood 75 feet in height. Each subsequent panel decreased in length as the steel-girdered pyramid rose. On January 29, the headtower stood over 260 feet tall and "steel monkey men" bolted in the number six panel girders. Girders weighed 40 to 50 tons. A powerful crane, working from the center of the headtower raised the huge girders slowly, while observers at selected points watched for problems.

A Southern Pacific train emerges from the railroad by-pass tunnel.

At the same time, the aggregate plant in Redding moved into operational status. Piles of different-size aggregate and sand accumulated, and the workers readied the blending tunnel conveyor. It would be here that inspectors would mix the appropriate ratio of different-size aggregate before placing the mix on the main conveyor belt heading to the dam site. Once the operation started at the Kutras aggregate plant, consultants arrived and checked the progress. In addition to Lowry's almost daily visits, Walker

R. Young, Supervising Engineer for the Central Valley Project reviewed operations. He met with a visiting team of consulting engineers from Stanford, the University of California, and Columbia University. Lowry called for a special meeting of consulting engineers and Bureau inspectors on January 31. Three high-ranking officials from the Bureau office in Denver joined the above-mentioned group of academic engineers. After touring the facilities at the Kutras site, the talented group of engineers poured over technical plans for the next important stage of dam construction, placing the concrete.

Good weather allowed extra work crews to begin installing the aggregate conveyor belt receiving station at the dam site. The belt, 36 inches wide, consisted of a special six-ply fabrication. Goodyear Rubber Company, already providing truck tires for the Shasta Dam job, hoped to gain worldwide recognition by having produced the world's longest conveyor belt.

An inspector checking the conveyor belt rollers

Crews worked so fast that hardly anyone noticed the changing weather. By mid-February the rain began to fall, almost daily. Starting on February 26 and lasting for three days, it poured. On that first day six inches fell in just over four hours! The streams rose, dumping more and more water into the rapidly rising Sacramento River. Crowe and Lowry quietly hoped and prayed for the deluge to stop. Their worry centered not so much on the rising river, but on the loose muddy ground. Heavy construction work is difficult even under dry conditions. With the knee-deep mud, workers could not be expected to produce quality work, and safety

Truck bridge washed out during flood

became an issue. However, Crowe had more than mud to worry about. By the morning of the 27th PCI officials measured the now-raging Sacramento River at 135,000 cubic feet per second at the dam site. The downpour continued. News came from upstream that the Pit River and Bully Hill Bridges were threatened, and Crowe realized that his operations were also vulnerable. The low-lying Kutras aggregate site in Redding quickly flooded; the operation shut down by noon.

Nearby Redding residents, particularly farmers with scores of cattle grazing along the river channel nervously herded their stock to higher ground. Hundreds of curiosity seekers hurried down to the eroding river banks. Sporting umbrellas and rain coats these people braved the absolute drenching rain to watch the flood. Everyone knew it was a big one. First, branches of trees floated by, then timber from someone's home or barn. Others spotted cattle and chickens, most dead, some still struggling to survive. The initial excitement of observing a flood first-hand gave way to terror. The rain continued.

The rain stopped briefly on the morning of the 28th, yet the accumulated flow past the dam site ballooned to over 185,000 cubic feet per second (cfs), a record. Damage reports slowly came in. At the dam site fully one-third of the truck bridge had been ripped from its foundation and carried downstream. The diversion channel no longer existed, and the preliminary excavation of the powerhouse foundation sat submerged more than ten feet. The aggregate conveyor belt bridge at Coram disappeared, only the foundation piers remained.

Water rising at the aggregate plant in Redding

Redding was a disaster. The Kutras aggregate plant looked more like a giant lake. Damage proved extensive. Little could be done until the water receded.

The weather cleared on March 2 allowing PCI officials an opportunity to gage the full extent of the wreckage. A 50-yard wide gap had been ripped through the conveyor belt bridge at the Kutras site. Giant cranes, used to dragline gravel listed and sank in the mucky river bottom.

The primary gravel crusher itself had been crushed and destroyed. The remains of 24 tourist cabins and other privately owned buildings lie scattered around the Kutras tract aimlessly floating about. The main highway bridge into Redding also sustained significant damage. Entire concrete foundations, ripped out of the bedrock by the raging river, littered the river's edge along with twisted and mangled steel girders. Workers used the clearing skies to begin the arduous task of cleaning up the debris throughout a two mile stretch of the Sacramento River. Workers engaged in repair operations noticed at least 20 bloated cattle carcasses littering the Kutras Tract area.

Crowe ordered two special work crews to immediately repair the torn-away truck bridge at the dam site. The bridge was critical to continued progress; it allowed for the transportation back and forth between the east and west abutments. Temporary scaffolding allowed for foot traffic to cross the bridge. Within two weeks replacement girders arrived from Ohio and full scale

The conveyor belt back in operation after the flood

repairs moved ahead. By the end of March, the Kutras aggregate plant resumed preparation for sending gravel to the dam site, and the various bridges had been repaired. But, for those who lived the "great flood of 1940" there will never be another like it.

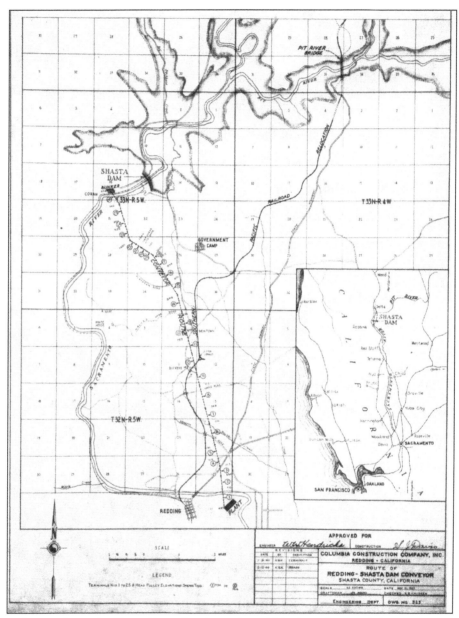

This map shows the Shasta Dam site, the projected lake boundary, and the conveyor belt route from Redding.

The cement, which came by train from San Jose, was held in these silos and then sent to the mixing plant near the headtower (far right).

Chapter 5
1941

All through early January waters of the Sacramento River remained high, curtailing work in the old riverbed and on some portions of the powerhouse. Work focused on continuing to place the concrete on the foundation of the dam itself, both on the east and west abutments. During this month Goodyear Tire and Rubber Company sent H.B. Brownell to Shasta Dam. The talented filmmaker visited every component of the Shasta Dam construction filming a motion picture to be released for educational purposes. Brownell saw drainage pumps working desperately to vacate the water around the flooded powerhouse foundation works. He filmed all stages of concrete placing and he caught glimpses of daring "rigger" men dangling high above the work site, inspecting cables.

Meanwhile, at the Redding Kutras aggregate plant, repairmen worked hard to replace damaged and completely wrecked machinery, victims of the December 1940 flood. Construction crews in this low lying area of the Sacramento River continually had to deal with quickly rising waters that appeared to recede just as quickly. Working in one spot for more than a few hours during the whole month of January proved difficult as the rains continued to come down. Flood damage to the south Kutras tract widened the riverbed more than one hundred feet, unprecedented in recorded history. Many of the newly acquired dragline shovel cranes, responsible for dredging gravel from the Sacramento River bed, had to be withdrawn to locations higher in elevation. This proved annoying, as the best samples of pre-selected gravel size and sand deposits were located in the riverbed. Luckily Crowe and Lowry had planned for extensive reserves already deposited in huge piles at the dam site.

A general view of the cement silos and the Coram gravel plant. The truck bridge is seen at the far right.

One of the most interesting aspects of the early stages of concrete placing involved the extensive use of reinforcement iron bars in the powerhouse and in the inspection galleries. Miles of heavy gauge rebar lined the inspection galleries alone. PCI foremen inspected the placement of the grid-like rebar system constantly, checking for proper connections and shifting seams. Even more difficult was the manner in which the workers had to move about. The rebar proved heavy enough for workers to climb on thus forming a ladder-like web throughout the concrete forming areas. Yet, one slip and a worker could lose several weeks work, out with a sprained or broken foot. Each gallery block presented peculiar problems. Some of the blocks had extra lengths of cooling tubing, while others had electrical connections. The galleries 7 feet in height and 5 feet in width would provide access to inspect the interior portions of the dam. Huge cranes placed the gallery sections, already pre-poured concrete forms, with great precision. Workers then ribbed the galleries with 2-inch thick industrial rebar providing a solid joint connection once the main concrete placing began over the top of the gallery form.

Concrete block forms

Like a conductor of a great orchestra the headtower foremen coordinated the placement of each bucket of concrete. The timing was critical. While one bucket was being withdrawn back to the headtower and lowered to receive a new 8-yard load of freshly mixed concrete, another bucket moved out from the headtower. By February, with the river still high and gushing between the east and west abutments, concrete placement increased on the west abutment. A large contractor's layout board detailing the sequence of concrete placement stood down at the foremen's headquarters. Here Crowe, Lowry, Bureau inspectors, and PCI foremen checked the progress at each numbered foundation block.

Now the operation at Shasta Dam swung into full gear. As March appeared, even though waters remained high around the powerhouse, crews went to work erecting forms and preparing for concrete placement. Scores of newly hired men went to work on the west abutment foundation blocks. Crews were expanded so that operations could continue at full speed during the swing shift and into the night. Well-placed floodlights

The first bucket of concrete

allowed crews to inspect the day's concrete placement and construct new concrete forms for the next day's work. Hundreds of men worked on each shift. Around the middle of March additional men came on-board to construct a huge shop building at the Coram site. Here the giant 15-foot diameter penstocks would be fabricated.

April of 1941 stands out as a banner month, not only was dam construction in full swing but the neighboring communities blossomed. With employment opportunities on the rise, the dam area communities celebrated the spring weather. The Shasta Cascade Wonderland Association sponsored a program of luncheons, activities, and contests. One of the highlights of the celebration, the Miss Alice of

Wonderland contest drew large crowds to the Toyon Community Center. At the same time the Mutual Broadcasting Company arrived at the dam site. Their plans called for a coast-to-coast broadcast. Nationally known commentator John B. Hughes interviewed Crowe as to the progress on the dam. He asked the superintendent if the dam would be completed within the designated time and if hiring would continue. Also interviewed on the broadcast was cableway operator Bill Ross and Mrs. Ross. Other announcers such as Mel Venter and A.W. Scott toured the site interviewing workers and foremen.

With over one hundred feet high of the foundation placing already in place it became necessary to regularly

Workers placing concrete, while inspectors check the operation

check the condition of the setting concrete. Information needed to be gathered on the seals and joints; these were observable from the numerous interior galleries. Specially trained inspectors moved through the galleries, block by block, checking critical joints for movement, water leakage, and cracks. Every day inspectors also moved across the exterior face and finish of the dam foundation. Likewise, after every concrete placement within the blocks, workers checked the condition of the drying concrete immediately following the tamping procedure. After the inspection of the exterior surface, special concrete finishers moved over the block face and cemented a smooth finish to the rough puck-marked surface. This procedure of final finishing, known as "sackrubbed finishing," provided a finished seal coat. By April 7, 1941, more than 800,000 yards of concrete had already been placed.

On May 3 of that year, the first millionth cubic yard of concrete was placed. While few officials from the Bureau or PCI were on hand that afternoon on block 29-E, construction "stiffs" were excited that a landmark had been reached. Early problems coordinating the cableway system had by now, been worked out. Visiting observers noted an efficient coordination of all phases of dam building. Powerplant construction soared as the weather dried in May. More and more men joined in the building. Both the oil storage tanks and the powerplant service bays were installed.

With the increase of so many new men on the job, it became difficult to maintain a clean safety record. While the number of fatalities, injuries, and accidents were well documented--and criticized--on the Hoover Dam job, Crowe

The headtower set for operation

and Lowry were determined to not have a repeat at Shasta Dam. But, accidents do happen; and happen they did at Shasta Dam. Numerous cases of individual and group bravery in rescuing and assisting the injured had already occurred. On May 10 of 1941 Ralph Lowry presented the National Safety Council President's Medal to three men who assisted in the saving of B.S. Hodges on October 20, 1940. Hodges, working at the Coram tract hopper, became buried in a small discharge gate after a cave in. George Base, Columbia Construction Co. employee, and Mark Whitaker, a Pacific Constructors workman, extricated Hodges. Standing nearby N.A. Takala, of the Bureau of Reclamation, rushed to the side of Hodges and successfully revived him through the use of artificial respiration. Scores of newly hired men, to help promote proper safety measures, worked alongside veteran dam builders. All were required to wear hard hats, gloves, and industrial strength work clothing. As the weather warmed, this proved uncomfortable. Many men preferred to wear a heavy duty brand of overalls. All wore heavy duty boots.

Always concerned about safety, PCI and Bureau personnel encouraged innovative methods to keep safety on the minds of the workers. In June of 1941 everyone

Safety awards presented to the men who helped save a fellow worker, B. S. Hodges

welcomed the initiation of a new monthly newsletter dedicated to exchanging ideas of safety techniques and to report on accidents. Called *The Headtower*, the publication grew in popularity quickly. Editor-in-Chief, Gene Green, explained the newsletter's purpose as "...we hope to reduce accident rates and encourage safety at Shasta Dam." He went on to acknowledge that all large construction jobs are prone to "some injuries," but if workers adhere closely to mandated safety rules and regulations, unnecessary accidents can be avoided. Ralph Lowry, applauded Green's attempt to reduce injuries stating, "The publication will be a distinct factor in maintaining and promoting safe working conditions at Shasta Dam." One of the first pieces of advice in the first issue of *The Headtower* included an article by John E. Kirkpatrick, Chief Surgeon at the Shasta Dam Hospital. He warned the men to beware of heat exhaustion working in the extremely hot summer months. Among other medicinal remedies, the doctor urged the men to consume "a tablespoon of Karo Syrup in a glassful of water before going to work, repeating at lunch and after arriving home." Superintendent Crowe also was eager to see the newsletter succeed, "If the publication 'Head Tower' will be successful in preventing just one serious accident, it will have served its purpose. I hope all our men will read it carefully, because none of us are too old to learn. I want you all to know that our accident prevention activities have always had my wholehearted approval, and I look to all of you to continue to do your part in carrying out our safety program."

Shasta Dam Hospital

The Shasta dam hospital was one of the best built, equipped and staffed hospitals in the northern part of California. The basic design of the hospital, its facilities and equipment were planned by John E. Kirkpatrick, M.D. and Daniel M. Brown, R.N. The new hospital was air conditioned and equipped with the latest devices medical science had produced. The building was long and rectangular in shape with the out-patient activities grouped at one end and the in-patients at the other. The administration and physicians' offices occupied the center. On the main floor were four private rooms, a 24-bed ward, a 12-bed ward, utility rooms, kitchen and dining room—all grouped so that out-patients could be cared for, with no traffic through the hospital proper. In the basement was an examining room and quarters for the nursing staff.

Green asked W. A. Dexheimer, Chief Bureau Inspector, to describe the importance and the purpose of building Shasta Dam. Green felt that it would be beneficial for everyone working on the project to know about the impact the dam would have. Dexheimer claimed that Shasta reservoir would back up for 35 miles, creating a large new recreational area. He went on stating that the dam will "regulate the flow of the Sacramento River for navigation improvement, flood control, irrigation, and salinity repulsion, maintaining a more uniform flow throughout the year." He stressed that cities and factories will also benefit from the hydroelectric power that will be produced.

The first issue of the newsletter announced the formation of baseball and softball leagues. Five teams were named for the types of work its players engaged in. They included the Cleanup, Engineers, Pipefitters, Inspectors, and Office. One team, called "Okies," was comprised of veteran dam builders that traced their work on dams back through Parker and Hoover Dams to the Midwest. These games, played at Toyon and other hastily roughed out fields, became a source of gratifying entertainment for players and their families. Dozens of spectators, toting snacks and drinks, cheered on their teams every Monday, Wednesday, and Friday evenings. By the end of 1941 newly installed bleachers attested to the growing popularity of the competition.

The Mutual Broadcasting program, numerous newspaper accounts, and continuing news releases by the Bureau of Reclamation, all helped to bring many new visitors to the dam site. In June hundreds of visitors came

---

Toyon Softball

Six teams were entered in the softball league in Toyon with games starting at 6:30 p.m. The schedule for the next week is:

July 16 Cleanup vs Engineers
July 18 Inspectors vs Pipefitters
July 21 Engineers vs Pipefitters
July 23 Inspectors vs Okies
July 25 Cleanup vs Office

Anyone wanting to play softball or hardball should turn out. Watch for the Baseball Dance soon!
                        --Headtower News

daily. An expanded parking lot held dozens of cars and busses. Special groups, particularly educational classes, came to see the giant dam. All the way from Montana, where giant Fort Peck (an earth fill dam) was being built, came the Senior class of the Montana School of Mines.

The Kutras gravel pit continued to provide a seemingly inexhaustible supply of aggregate. A giant powerful "grizzly and jaw crusher" installed earlier, crushed raw deposits of riverbed material. Sorting screens then

separated the material into .75 inch and 1.50 inch size limits. Conveyor belt in operation
The resulting gravel, moved onto the ten mile conveyor belt, heading north to the Coram transfer site. The belt crossed the Sacramento River twice and Highway 99 once. Special splash guards prevented rocks from falling down onto passing automobiles. The highway crossing boasted a sign

71

advertising to the passing public that this was the world's longest conveyor belt.

July witnessed the arrival of the first 15-foot diameter penstock section at the Coram fabrication plant. A monstrous 80-ton press held the plate steel sections as experienced welders, sweating from July temperatures and heat emitted from the arc-welders, seared the joints closed. Other workers, using heavy-duty grinders, smoothed end sections and prepared for the joining of another section. The penstocks, once installed, would bring rushing water from midway down the dam to the power turbines. Due to increased pressure of the funneled water at the lower end of the penstocks, engineers designed the lower sections to be stronger. They accomplished this by increasing the thickness of the

You could literally drive a truck through the penstock

steel plate, which was of the highest quality obtainable, for the final penstock sections entering the powerhouse.

Finally, hot July and August weather dried the lower old Sacramento River bed. Draining water from both sides of the abutments had been spilling into this lower area.

72

Now crews safely moved into the riverbed, setting forms for the dam foundation. Since this would be the lowest point, excavation needed to go deep to find bedrock. Here the width of the dam would be greatest. Cableway cranes hoisted 40-foot concrete forms into place as men scrambled to set each section. With so much loading, unloading, and handling of heavy equipment, it was only a matter of time before an accident would occur. Crowe knew this and he constantly reviewed safety procedures with his safety committee and each foreman. Despite these precautions, a dam worker died, crushed at the headtower loading dock. The August 7 fatality forced Crowe and Lowry to call another special safety meeting. It was decided that any worker found to be not following proper safety procedures would lose his job immediately. Part of

Wearing hardhats was required--here a worker briefly takes it off.

the ruling demanded that hard hat, gloves, and safety goggles must be worn (where designated) even though brutal summer temperatures climbed past the century mark. Disaster almost struck again on August 13 when a rock slide swept away two conveyor belt foundation piers near the headtower. Crews working below the slide scurried to the side, abandoning trucks and equipment.

Just four days later a radio team of Columbia Broadcasting System (CBS) personnel arrived to air a national program on work progress. The team included:

Will Thompson, Robert LeMond, and Tro Harper (announcers); Jim French (engineer); Fox Case (producer), and a very young Chet Huntley (program director). On the afternoon of August 17, Huntley went on the air with a coast-to-coast live update. Throughout the rest of the day and into the evening, Huntley and his announcers roamed the work site interviewing PCI personnel, Bureau inspectors, and regular construction "stiffs." Lowry, dressed for the occasion, read from a prepared script. He reviewed the progress and talked about meeting the completion schedule. No references were made of the recent accidents, although he assured the radio audience that all precautions were being taken. LeMond, wearing a hard hat and overalls, went into the "pits," where he reported on the concrete placing routine during an actual pour. Meanwhile, colleague Tro Harper, interviewed "Happy" Hepner, a hoist operator.

Safety was always an issue, especially in situations such as shown in this photo--with men working at the top of the headtower.

Safety became a major concern again in August as *The Headtower* gloomily announced that the number of lost-time accidents for July had risen to 58. A chart showing the fluctuating nature of lost time accidents revealed that safety standards needed to be strongly enforced. Much of the responsibility was placed on the job foremen. It was suggested that "One of the shortcomings of some foremen's supervision is their

74

inability to concentrate on unsafe practices and to exercise sufficient imagination to foresee the consequences of conditions that are sometimes complicated and obscure." Large numbers of injuries occurred during the concrete bucket placement. No matter how much you prepared for the load, men would need to scurry about attending to last minute details, causing confusion and rushing. The August issue of the newsletter announced the beginning of a new set of safety hand signals that all concrete foremen, spotters, and crane operators must adhere to. A tapping of the hardhat meant headtower, tapping rear-end signalled the tailtower, thumbs down meant "crack" (open slightly) the concrete bucket, while thumbs up called for the full dumping of the concrete. Other signals gave directions on exact bucket placement. Foremen were expected to only dump concrete loads after site preparation had been completed and exact dumping site had been determined. A quick survey of hospital reported visits showed that men were jumping off of moving vehicles, dumping concrete loads haphazardly, using makeshift ladders, boards with nails were left lying about and sandblasters were not wearing safety goggles. In fact, reported eye injuries ranked high every month.

Workers standing on a large platform, suspended by a cable from the headtower

While the safety committee worried about lost time injuries, they proudly displayed the construction achievement records through July. The record showed that 2.5 million pounds of powder had been exploded using

590,000 blasting caps, 5,317,633 linear feet (1007 miles) of blasting holes had been drilled, 21.9 miles of cableway had been rigged, and 2,2256,400 feet (427 miles) of cooling pipe had been installed. The committee calculated that 5000 men had been issued hardhats, with 2000 of them also given safety belts for scaling steep inclines. Over 2000 pairs of goggles and 3000 pairs of safety boots had also been issued. The medical department announced that over 7000 men had applied for positions on the dam and that PCI had expended more than $7 million in wages.

Diverting the water of the Sacramento River forced Crowe and Lowry to plan carefully for the expected high

Pumping water from the riverbed into the diversion channel

water levels of the rainy season. Beginning in August, crews worked to build diversion walls, timber cribs, and dirt coffer dams. All of these devices, built in steps, would effectively change the course of the river in order to allow dry access of the old riverbed. *Headtower* editor, Gene Green described the diversion technique for all of the workers.

> The first step, of course, is to provide a channel for the river which will allow the unexcavated area to be completely exposed. To do this, it is necessary to build three walls, designated above as Walls No.1, No.2, and No.3. No. I wall is a thin reinforced concrete wall along the east side of the 43 row extending downstream from block 430 and connecting with Wall No.2 which is a rock-filled timber crib. Wall No.3, also a reinforced concrete wall, fills up the remaining gap by closing from the east side of Block 42A to a rock point just upstream.

76

After all these walls are constructed and the concrete in rows 42, 43, 44, and 45 are brought up to the proper elevation as indicated on each block in the sketch, the upstream coffer dam will be broken and another coffer dam built across the present diversion channel just above the coffer dam bridge. Final closure will be made by another rock-filled coffer dam in the present diversion channel at a point about opposite the powerhouse.

Muck excavated from the remaining spillway section can be hauled out over these last two coffer dams.

The year 1941 proved to be a popular year for visitors. In October, Secretary of the Interior Harold Ickes, his wife, and other government officials checked-in for several days. Ickes, sporting a heavy overcoat, surveyed the operations at several sites around the dam. He approved of the work progress, congratulating Crowe, Lowry, and Bureau Commissioner John C. Page. Of particular interest to Ickes was the Visitor Center and Vista House. The working model of Shasta Dam and the panoramic Central Valley Project model appeared to serve as positive publicity for this New Deal program. Ickes also saw the first welded penstock tubing sections being placed on the dam. He worried about the narrow diversion channel. Ickes had been told of the great 1940 flood and he

Visitor Observation Gallery

queried Crowe and Lowry on their contingency plans should the quickly approaching winter season bring another deluge. Lowry pointed out that work was progressing well on the lowest portion of the old Sacramento River bed spillway and that water could be diverted through this area and the railroad by-pass tunnel shortly. On November 13, buckets of concrete began arriving at forms in the spillway foundation area.

October's safety news brought a sharp reaction from editor, Gene Green. Increased eye injuries due to men not wearing goggles seemed to be easily avoided, and Green let everyone know it.

Those who would command, must first learn to obey. It is difficult to understand the attitude of a great many of our employees who deliberately jeopardize their eyesight by failure to wear goggles. Scarcely a day goes by, but that it is necessary to warn some workman, especially in the clean up gangs, to wear his goggles. Time after time we have observed these men holding a gad [conversation] while doing rock chipping work, their eyes exposed to the most serious type of eye injury, and still we see their goggles on their hats or around their neck. Last month we had a total of almost twenty eye injuries, the over-whelming majority of which were caused by out and out failure and indifference toward this goggle problem.

Your eyesight is a precious thing and there is no remedy for vision once destroyed. No where are there spare parts to be procured to remedy your damaged vision. When this job is over you men will probably have to pass a physical examination when you seek employment elsewhere and impaired vision is at the top of the list these days as a cause for rejection for employment.

Goggles are available to every workman whose duties require him to work under circumstances where his eyesight is in jeopardy. We cannot stand over every man to enforce discipline, but we can do something about it, if this flagrant disregard of our safety orders about goggles is continued. The decision is up to you.

To help drive home the safety point Green began citing each reported accident, withholding names but identifying the type of job being performed, how the accident happened and the resulting loss in wages to the worker.

While the concrete crews worked around the clock to pour the foundation in the spillway forms, the rains became more and more frequent. By December 3, the Sacramento River crested at 30,000 cfs. All work in the spillway foundation area had to be curtailed, and men and machinery evacuated. Luckily, at the powerhouse, the foundation and the first two levels had been completed. Here work continued.

The morning after Pearl Harbor, Bureau photographer T.B. Gibson busied himself taking pictures of the hastily placed guards. Worried that Japanese living in California might attempt to sabotage the work on Shasta Dam, government and military officials ordered soldiers to protect strategic and vital operations at the dam. Crowe and Lowry did not object. They agreed that it would not take more than a handful of armed guards to protect key areas. Guards were added to all entry points, at the gravel plant, and at the railroad by-pass tunnel. Other soldiers cruised up and down the 10-mile dirt road that paralleled the aggregate conveyor belt. Gibson hurried on to the hospital where his schedule called for a complete photo

Soldier guarding the railroad by-pass tunnel

layout of the Shasta Dam Hospital. Ironically, just previous to his visit several injured dam workers had been released and when Gibson shot the hospital ward, few beds were occupied. The hospital, claimed to be the best equipped and staffed north of Sacramento, contained its own kitchen, a convalescing ward, a clinical laboratory, minor and major

79

surgery rooms, administrative offices, and a nursing station. Under John C. Kirkpatrick, the dedicated and talented staff handled all worker injuries. On occasion, dependents of dam workers, admitted under a special participation plan, used the facilities.

War news spread through the boomtown communities, Toyon, and Shasta Dam Village quickly. Rumors spread that a Japanese invasion was imminent and that the

Children of dam workers playing in the snow during the winter of 1941-42

dam would be bombed as soon as Japanese planes came within range. Men discussed the possibility of enlisting, wondering how long the war would take, and if their job on the dam would still be available when they returned. And even though minor flood water repeatedly swept through the dam area, PCI foremen pushed their men to work harder. The government was already telling them that the expected water-generated electricity would be needed for America's war effort. As Christmas approached dam workers and their families gave thanks for their relative prosperity and prayed for a quick end to the war.

Chapter 6
1942

1942 started off on a nervous and apprehensive note. Everyone was concerned about the war. What would happen next? Would they pull us all off the Shasta job and ask us to fight? What would become of our families? If we did leave, could we get our jobs back after the war? These and other tough questions were being asked by hundreds of workers as they reported to jobs in January. Crowe and Lowry did not have all the answers. Their only concern remained, to complete the dam on schedule and for bid-cost. The men had a difficult time keeping their minds on their work. Every day, war news drifted through the work area. Rumors of imminent Japanese invasion pervaded most of the conversation. Others seemed concerned that the war would be over before they had an opportunity to fight.

As the men worried about the future of their jobs and their families, they worked in increasingly colder weather. Record low temperatures hit in January and three-foot icicles hung from wooden platforms and from concrete forms. Sporting shirts, overalls, gloves, and heavy work coats, they tried their best to complete tasks. Injuries occurred with men slipping and stumbling on glassy concrete surfaces. Crowe had a notion to curtail work, but he knew time lost is difficult to regain. The word was sent out by the safety committee that all men were to slow their work, taking extra precautions.

Down at Coram, the fabrication of the penstock sections moved ahead briskly. Additional welding crews started to join the 15-foot sections together and ready them for placement in the dam. Welders enjoyed the extra heat,

Checking welding joints with an X-Ray machine

and they happily chided their friends who had to work outside in the ice and snow. Two special X-Ray machines arrived. Technicians used these devices to check the quality of the welded joints, both on the inside and outside. The outside X-Ray machine was quite large and could examine a three-foot linear zone. The penstock sat on large rollers and was rotated with each new photograph. In this manner the entire circumference could be checked. Meanwhile, on the inside of the penstock, men used a smaller X-Ray device to check interior welds. The process involved specially trained technicians who examined the X-Rays immediately following film development. They then reported to the fabrication foremen on the acceptability of the weld.

If the welding inspection went well, approved penstock sections were loaded onto flatbed trailers and driven to the dam. Here riggers fastened cables from the headtower and signaled the ground level operator who then called up to the headtower operator. The giant tubing was now lifted and placed onto temporary wooden cradles.

Penstock sections set on wooden cradles

In March, Lowry was informed that local Indians were upset about the possibility of flooding the Curl Cemetery. The cemetery had been a traditional burial site and was still held in high regard. Not wanting to create a situation and in complete compliance, Lowry offered to send a work crew out to the cemetery and re-inter the bodies to other locations. This decision and the offer of help satisfied Indian leaders, and the work was carried out without incident.

At the same time, an unexpected March snowfall covered the dam area. Kids in the boomtowns built snowmen and engaged in snowball fights, while their fathers drearily reported to work. Actually, the snow did not accumulate deep, and within days work production returned to normal levels. By the end of March, with work in full swing, the three-millionth cubic yard of concrete was ceremoniously placed. This event signaled the half-way point in concrete placing; yet, much work lay ahead and the pressing need to get the turbines generating electricity remained.

Much of the work at Shasta Dam relied on the constant use of cables. Cables lifted just about everything over one hundred pounds. They varied in size from .5-inch truck cables and small machinery cables, to the massive three-inch main headtower cables. Cableway "monkeys" risked life and limb in a constant survey of cable conditions. Worn or deteriorating cables needed repair immediately. On more than one occasion the main headtower cables broke under the strain of carrying tons of concrete. Lashing down like a giant whip the dangerous cable ends sent nearby workers scurrying for cover. At least once, severe injuries occurred when a broken cable hit a cement finisher, flicking him from the supporting scaffolding like an enormous

The 3-Millionth yard of concrete being placed

horsetail lashing a fly. The machine shop busied itself repairing cables and returning them to active service.

Visitors to the site during the month of April saw a rapidly rising concrete dam. Both the east and west concrete abutment were impressively high. All five penstocks rested in their foundations awaiting final hook-up to the power generation plant. Across the river, the power transmission yard began to take shape as large capacity transformers sat ready for installation. Yet, much work remained, and with the manpower shortage Crowe and Lowry concerned themselves with long-range completion dates. To help deal with the manpower shortage Master Mechanic, Red Malan designed a one-man pneumatic concrete vibrator. He wanted a device that would be as effective as the old two-man model. By the end of April, several of Malan's vibrators began operating on the east abutment. The machine worked well, and soon others were brought into use.

One-man concrete vibrator

Still worried about manpower shortages, Crowe authorized a search for additional workers. Most able bodied men in the boomtowns and in Redding, had already enlisted for military service or moved to the Bay Area for high paying defense related jobs. There, thousands found lucrative employment at Kaiser's shipyards in Richmond and Alameda. Others went to Los Angeles or San Diego and worked in aircraft plants. Empty boomtown homes increased and Crowe decided to extend his search to the Sacramento area. There "recruiters" convinced unemployed men, many of them Mexican, to try a job at Shasta Dam. Few actually could be convinced, and those that did arrive, soon left the area once they saw the danger involved in much of the labor.

Crowe had other concerns that kept him occupied for most of May. He knew the importance of keeping the correct temperature for the massive concrete monolith he was building. The plans had originally called for 1-inch

copper cooling pipe to be installed five feet apart for every layer of concrete placing. Cool 50° F. Sacramento River water, pumped through the pipes helped in the curing process. However, Bureau inspectors noticed that the initial blocks revealed

Laying out the concrete cooling pipes

uneven curing and considerable stress. Engineers recommended that the pumped water needed to be colder. A warehouse-size refrigeration plant was then constructed. Located at the base of the east abutment, it helped to super cool water to a temperature of 35° F. before being passed through the cooling pipes. The downstream face of the quickly rising dam became dotted with cooling system headers, risers, and coil connections. The lines needed to be checked constantly for leaks. In the refrigeration plant controllers monitored operating temperatures on the main condenser and closely watched the condition of the cooling pumps. Since concrete takes a long time to cure, these special cooling arrangements prevented structural stress and cracking.

On the upstream face of the dam new energy and effort began on the construction of the "trashracks." Long cylindrical concrete protuberances, the trashracks were designed to screen debris from entering each of the penstocks. With the warm dry weather of June extra crews went to work setting concrete forms and installing reinforcement bars. Working on the upstream face of the dam proved to be a completely different experience from the sloped

Trashracks are clearly seen in this phase of construction

downstream side. Looking straight down the vertical side unnerved some workers as they struggled with heavy equipment and unwieldy hand tools. The men adjusted within days, displaying their agility on narrow catwalks, vertical ladders, and temporary platforms.

From their vantage point hundreds of feet above the upstream slope, workers on the trashracks watched as dump truck after dump truck carted in land fill in an attempt to create a cofferdam in the river channel. This would funnel the Sacramento along the western abutment, and give workers the opportunity to begin pouring concrete blocks in the old river channel. Digging deep into the old channel, excavators carved out rectangular depressions that would become the foundation of the most central portion of the dam and the spill way. Viewed from the top of the 460-foot

The scale and difficulty of the construction awed many visitors.

headtower, workers in the river channel appeared as so many ants scurrying about, while giant bulldozers looked like tinker toys. From the vantage point of the channel, men looked upward and nervously eyed the concrete wall that held back the rapidly flowing Sacramento River. The proportions and scale of the entire scene must have humbled the proudest of men. Yet, here was man, changing the course of a mighty river at will, and erecting a 600-foot high concrete structure that would last for thousands of years.

To measure the amount of stress and strain on the newly placed concrete, a series of strain meters were installed at strategic locations. The extremely sensitive devices measured lateral and vertical pressure. Minute movements could then be correlated over time to give structural engineers an idea of what the mass of surrounding concrete was doing. In addition, a number of joint meters recorded expansion and contraction of each blocked concrete section. At regular intervals inspectors checked the meter, recorded computations and discussed overall concrete behavior. Depending on the readings, officials could adjust the flow and temperature of cooling pipes in the problem area.

With little or no ceremony, construction "stiffs" dumped the 4-millionth yard of concrete into a form on August 31, 1942. Down in the riverbed diversion, foremen consulted with Bureau inspectors as they calculated the river diversion schedule. Timing was important. Constantly changing river levels compounded the calculations. Row gates diverted the Sacramento River, either along the east or west abutments.

Alternating the river flow between center blocks

Then workers scrambled to place concrete on the drying row. This system of alternating river flow and concrete placement appeared to work well throughout September, and the blocks rose higher and higher in the river bed channel. Now the idea was to allow the water to flow through a single row block, #44. A series of 5-foot steps or jumps formed a fish ladder in the channel, allowing the passing of salmon upstream. In this way, the rest of the lower channel bed could be prepared for concrete. Eventually, the plan called for raising the river water level 70 feet and then diverting the river through the railroad by-pass tunnel.

The year 1942 ended with work crews preparing to reinforce and concrete the south portal of the railroad by-

pass tunnel, preparing it to receive the diverted Sacramento River. The spillway section rose over 100 feet, the powerhouse structure neared completion, the penstocks approached the powerhouse, the east abutment climbed passed the 500-foot mark in elevation, and the west abutment rose over 400 feet. One could see that construction progress had been impressive, even under the challenging engineering pressures and the troubling early war period.

Final diversion tunnel preparations

90

The headtower is shown here in full operation. Once work began on placing the concrete in their block forms, the cableway system remained in operation around-the-clock until late 1944.

A typical day in the construction work at Shasta Dam saw bucket after bucket of freshly mixed concrete delivered and placed into pre-fabricated forms. Workers stood nearby guiding the bucket to its final, exact destination. A worker then pulled the bucket release lever and the concrete dropped out. Next, the concrete was spread out and tamped down. Finally, workers used heavy-duty vibrating machines to compact the concrete.

Chapter 7
1943

War news in the early months of 1943 remained bleak with the Germans pushing closer to Moscow and Leningrad.   Out in the Pacific, American forces had apparently stopped the tide of Japanese aggression. However, we did not have the ability to take the offensive. Concern over the war prevailed in every aspect of work on the dam.   Men talked constantly about war progress wondering if any of their former dam working colleagues, were seeing any action. Women in the boomtowns formed wartime sewing clubs, getting together weekly to sew a wide variety of garments that could be used by soldiers. Children formed collection clubs, scouring the dam area for tin, rubber, glass, and other useful scraps. Toyon School curriculum focused on geography. Students mapped the war

fronts, keeping track of where American forces were engaged.

Crowe and Lowry, briefed regularly by Bureau officials on the need to generate power as soon as possible, moved to speed up the installation of power generating equipment. In January, scroll cases S-1 and S-2 were installed into their service bays in the powerhouse. The scroll case is the unit that accepts the inflowing lake waters. Vanes in the scroll case direct the water against the blades of the water wheel in the turbine and then discharge the water into the river. Built in sections and assembled with seals and gaskets, these units underwent pressure and leak testing before being lowered into the powerhouse.

Already in place and operating in the powerhouse was a 250-ton power crane. The large lift moved laterally across the entire main floor, providing unlimited access. Later, the crane would place all the necessary components to bring the powerhouse on-line, including the generators, main shafts, and electrical control panels. Electricians watched as over 20 power switching terminals were eased into place.

The powerhouse under construction

The seven foot high panels capable of handling over 2300 volts of water-generated power were connected to miles of heavy gage electrical wire.

Work moved along quickly on the installation of the scroll cases and other power generating equipment

94

throughout January and February. During this time the five millionth cubic yard of concrete was set down into a form. Unusually cold winter weather forced men to wear heavier clothing and warm their numbing hands. Cement "stiffs" concentrated their efforts on building up the center blocks of the spillway. Progress by March revealed that the four spillway blocks had been built up over 300 feet. Block row #44 remained as the funnel way for the Sacramento River. One other block was kept low in case flooding winter waters forced the use of additional diversion routes.

This night scene shows two of the open blocks where Sacramento River water flowed.

The low rainfall totals for the Spring of 1943 kept the Sacramento River manageable. Crews working on makeshift platforms on the upstream side of the spillway constantly looked at the river levels before commencing to complete the concrete trashracks. By April it was clear that the river would not flood and contingency flood plans were scrapped. On the west abutment the river diversion tunnel stood ready to accept the Sacramento River. Men prepared the north and south portal openings, laying concrete funnel channels.

Beginning in May temporary bulkhead gates placed into Block #40 diverted river water to Block #44. Inside Block #40 several work crews assembled concrete forms in preparation of intensive concrete pouring to raise this level. Working in a canyon-like setting with the west abutment rising more than 500 feet and the 100 foot spillway section enclosing them, the men labored in an effort to quickly raise this critical block. Crowe's intricate cableway system worked well in this confining space. Radio operators signaled to headtower operators constantly giving them instructions to lift lower, more to the right or left, etc. From the headtower little, if any, of the work in Block #44 could be seen.   .

On June 23, 1943, bulldozers broke open the upstream dirt coffer dam located near the upstream portal opening of the diversion tunnel. Sacramento River water gushed through the portal, slicing its way through the long tunnel shaft and emerged on the downstream side about a minute later. Men all over the dam paused to watch the cascading water run down the south portal channel and crash into the river. The water

This photo shows river water gushing through the diversion tunnel. Now, workers began placing concrete in the last remaining blocks.

level on the upstream side immediately went down, leaving open Block #40 dry. Now workers installed a temporary flood gate to keep back waters should the diversion tunnel fail to channel surges in water levels.

Additional work crews swarmed into Block #40 intending to raise this level as soon as possible. In perfect coordination, cableway operators lowered concrete, gallery forms, elevator forms, and river outlet conduits. The conduits, 8.5 feet in diameter, would control most of the post-construction water releases from Shasta Dam. Engineered to exacting specifications, the tubing contained special contraction joints designed to "bend" with the curing of the concrete.

Down in the powerhouse, installation of the penstocks resumed. Cranes placed the powerhouse penstock connectors on their foundations. Inside the powerhouse workers assembled and installed portions of the Unit #4 turbine, even though rumors abounded that the power generating equipment would not be fully installed. It appeared that a priority was given to Grand Coulee Dam. The powerhouse there had already been completed and government officials reasoned that the generators placed on-line at Grand Coulee could help supply electrical energy to the defense plants in and around Seattle as well as the Hannover Nuclear Plant.

A huge power generating rotor is being lowered into place.

From August through the rest of the year new work crews prepared the downstream spillway apron area for concrete finishing. Digging shovels loaded material from high areas onto dump trucks that redistributed the debris in low areas. Concrete placing of blocks in the spillway moved along quickly, as each block was reduced in size as the dam grew taller. During this entire procedure, no water could enter the area. The diversion tunnel continued to reroute several thousand cubic feet per second; the rest of the Sacramento River water soon backed up, a reservoir formed.

Security at the dam site remained tight during 1943. Passes were required for all workers, and visitors could only observe from the Vista House. Soldiers were replaced by a Bureau police force that roamed the entire dam checking limit fences for breaks. Wearing hard hats and sporting official enforcement badges, most of these older gentlemen never encountered trouble. They spent most of their time approving work passes at the different checkpoints.

During September, the Bureau lowered a power boat onto the quickly rising reservoir. Mainline crane #1 gently

Shasta Lake begins to fill as the center blocks are quickly raised.

set the boat down near the center of the spillway amid floating boards and other debris. This marked the first occasion of a power boat on the reservoir. Bureau photographer W. F. Richards used the boat to take pictures of the upstream face of the dam and shots of the inundated town of Kennett. Curious onlookers spotted the boat cruising around the fledgling lake throughout the rest of that fall.

Visitors noticed a concentration of men and machines near the center of the dam. Foremen, anxious to raise the central blocks to the already established level on each abutment, pushed their men to complete the job. There was some concern that approaching winter rains could overwhelm the capacity of the diversion operation causing

98

the reservoir level to rise too quickly, endangering work crews in the center blocks. Activity abounded also on the extreme end of each abutment where experienced "stiffs" dug out and prepared for the final foundation concrete pouring. Here the "cut" penetrated 40 to 50 feet into the side of each mountain slope. Extra rebar reinforcing would be placed here to anchor any lateral shifts caused by water pressure. Elsewhere, veteran dam workers had a difficult time reinforcing the penstock pedestals and framing concrete forms. The problem resulted from the nature of the unique shape of the pedestal and the steep sloping ground. Concrete forms needed to be well fastened and anchored in order to provide an unmovable concrete form. Part of the problem was satisfied by substituting heavier timber forms.

Frank Crowe (left) and Ralph Lowry (right) welcome Bureau engineer Walker Young to the Shasta Dam site.

Interior partitions and additional electrical panels, wiring, and generator frames all were installed in November and December. Across the river men worked hard to erect the basic steel frame complex that would support the large capacity electrical transmission lines. Work also continued on the main switchyard. Much of the electrical components including the internal wiring came from Westinghouse Electric Company. Men dwarfed by the multi-ton generators carefully and systematically assembled the generator rotors to exacting specifications.

The year ended with the placing of the six millionth cubic yard of concrete. Another special sign was made to advertise the event, but no official ceremonies occurred. Everyone knew that, by now, the dam was nearing completion. As the sixth millionth cubic yard dropped into place in the rising central block area, veteran dam workers estimated that the job would only take one more year of final concrete placing.

Concrete crews by the end of 1943 worked quickly and efficiently to raise the center blocks of concrete.

Chapter 8
1944

The final year of dam construction started amid a swirling snowstorm. Nearby residents in Redding, not familiar with heavy snowfalls struggled to keep their automobiles on the icy roads. Out at the dam site, most work crews ignored the falling flakes, pressing on with construction. Crowe was determined to keep his men on schedule and he ordered special shed roofs erected where dry working conditions were necessary. The blizzard knocked down several newly installed transmission line poles and wires. Emergency repair parties left the dam site in chained trucks and located the fallen structures; temporary repairs held the lines intact until the snow melted days later.

Lowry also worried at this time. A loose bolt was discovered on one of the guy rods used to anchor a newly arrived transformer. On top of this a tie rod, framing the main laminations of the generator core, bent out more than an inch causing lamination displacement. The entire transformer had to be "untanked," that is, lifted out of its supporting concrete bay holder and sent back for repair or replacement. This was another disappointing blow to Lowry's plan of having one or two generators on-line by the completion of the concrete placing.

Due to the additional water pressure found in the spillway apron area, engineers needed to constantly test the strength of the concrete being placed there. In the testing laboratory, technicians spent hours crushing apron samples. These samples averaged six inches wide by twelve inches high and were cylindrical in shape. These samples were given 20 to 30 days to dry before being placed in the "crusher." Most tests use 90,000 to 105,000 pounds of pressure on the concrete samples, with strength readings averaging 3300 to 3650 psi. These readings proved to be more than adequate for the stress factors encountered in the spillway apron.

Throughout World War II women were utilized in administrative positions, as shown here, and in food preparation at the mess hall.

With the shortage of men during World War II, both the Bureau of Reclamation and PCI hired women to fill vacant clerical and food service positions. At Bureau headquarters in Toyon women served as secretaries and assistants. At the dam site, women worked in the PCI headquarters, again engaging in office work. One woman, Opal Foxx, worked in the mess hall.

Concrete placing increased in the spillway apron during January and February. While finishers floated the main spillway pad, others placed the arch deflectors, concrete channel bars designed to soften the impact of falling water from the dam. The arch deflectors, approximately 15 feet long, stood near the end of the spillway apron and were constructed using an extra strong concrete mix. The spillway side walls, also made of fortified concrete rose at this same time. Built to accept the full force of the crashing Sacramento River, the channel side walls contained added layers of

An aerial view showing work on the spillway of Shasta Dam

steel reinforcement. Above the sidewalls, the canyon rock protruded adding a feeling of natural strength.

Everyday during good weather the Bureau powerboat cruised around the small reservoir corralling debris jamming up near the diversion tunnel or gathering at the base of the dam. Word came down from Bureau headquarters that the crew of the powerboat was to tow a newly constructed service barge up the rising reservoir to Kennett. Once there, they were ordered to burn any standing wood structures. First to go was the still standing Gold Nugget Cafe, a popular eatery during the heyday of the copper mining boom prior to World War I. The barge served so well as a base of operations for crews assigned to patrol the new lake, that Lowry ordered another barge constructed. By now everyone had abandoned Kennett, that is, all except Lawrence Bannon. He stubbornly held out. Securing a houseboat to reside in, Bannon commuted about Shasta reservoir in a small skiff. Government barge operators checked on Bannon every few days and he became a regular visitor to the dam.

Lawrence Bannon

February saw a temporary dirt cofferdam piled just below the powerhouse. This became necessary when winter water from the diversion tunnel began to back up into the spillway apron. With the cofferdam in place extra work crews confidently labored at a feverish pace to finish the entire spillway area. On February 4, with reservoir levels rising, the decision was made to open river outlet valves for tubes #2 and #3. Each of the 8.5-foot diameter tubes worked well, with no major reported leaks from within the dam. On the spillway side, thousands of gallons of white water cascaded down crashing into the apron. Plowing into the dirt cofferdam, the newly released reservoir water quickly overwhelmed the 20-foot high barrier, smashing through and linking up the Sacramento River. For many workmen and visiting family members this sight was moving and memorable.

Now came an important moment, the shutting of the service gates to the diversion tunnel. This procedure would effectively cutoff the diversion of the Sacramento River and place the full control of the reservoir on the dam and its outlet valves. Utilizing a custom designed hoist the gates were lifted into place, never to be opened again. As the diversion tunnel emptied, an elite crew was organized to move into the tunnel. Their assignment was interesting-- construct a massive concrete plug, sealing off the reservoir water forever. Strong timbers erected at the plug site shaped the concrete as it was pumped in over 1200 feet from the south portal. This became the world's longest concrete pumping operation!

In the powerhouse, the process of completing generator #4 moved along. Precise planning, with exact measurements were needed before any electrical generator installation and this job was no exception. Placing the rotor for generator #4 proved time consuming. The huge workshop crane loomed overhead as the operator lowered the two foot hook and men fastened it to the rotor connector. On command, the crane operator lifted the gigantic rotor, slowly swinging it into position over the foundation and gently lowered it into place. As it approached the assembly cage the powerful crane stopped.

In 1944 two generators were installed in the powerhouse.

Workers scurried around the full circumference of the rotor placing sensitive levels along the top edge. Coordinating the readings foremen determined the proper levels and motioned for the crane operator to continue to lower the rotor slowly. Once the rotor rested squarely and evenly on the generator supports the crane let loose, moving to bring the rotor cap, or upper bearing truss, into its position. From here, the cap was bolted down, sealed and secured.

Across the river the switch-yard transmission lines stretched south toward its first major destination, Oroville. The task of clearing a 30-foot path through the suggested

southern route strained men and machines. Between huge majestic oaks and countless thickets of manzanita brush, clusters of annoying poison oak grew in scattered clumps. Crews downed the oaks and were followed by caravans of veteran bulldozer crews who swept away the small low-lying vegetation.

Horses were used to help raise electrical transmission lines heading south from the dam site.

Now hole-diggers went to work drilling through the tough hardpan of Shasta and Tehama Counties. Next, long flatbed trucks conveyed the transmission poles to the irrespective holes. These portable heavy duty cranes picked up the long wooden supports and dropped them into place. Cross poles were erected in areas known to sustain high wind conditions. Through March electricians also strung the transmission lines, uncoiling the precious wires from 8-foot spools. In some cases where they could be used, horses successfully pulled the reels of transmission lines. Attached to "comealongs," the horses proved more than adequate in stringing operations. One by one, linemen systematically

106

moved from one group of poles to another securing transmission lines with the specified tension and installing insulators.

The rapidly rising water of the Shasta reservoir overwhelmed the base of the headtower in early March. The concrete mixing plant had to be relocated on higher ground along with all the accompanying equipment. The plan now called for a temporary catwalk to be strung from the old aggregate belt towers to the mid-level of the headtower. Reminiscent of a jungle canyon bridge, the catwalk swung laterally and vertically whenever men walked on it. Headtower cableway operators crossed over on this bridge, walking carefully, and reported to work. The headtower continued in its role of delivering concrete, only now, the cableway cranes picked up the concrete at a new concrete mixing location.

The rising waters of Shasta Lake engulfed the headtower. Workers used a "catwalk" to get to and from the huge structure.

Thousands of pieces of floating debris made their way down to the dam, there to be trapped and removed by Bureau men working on government barges. Everything conceivable ended up thumping against the dam. House timbers and dead tree branches were the most common. In at least three cases complete homes would meander down the waterway, with roofs fully intact! Curious spectators began showing up regularly at the left abutment edge of the dam looking for debris of any value. Government personnel finally had to restrict this area as the amount of debris piled up.

The powerhouse passed its first major hallmark on March 29, 1944, when service station generator #1 was placed on-line by Bureau Electrical Engineer Irving C. Harris. The generated power was used on location at the dam site, as the transmission lines were not yet completed. The excitement of generating their own power, quickly gave way to disappointment, when on April 13 the upper guide bearing failed forcing a complete shut-down of generator #1. Powerhouse technicians were amazed to see the deep scoring in the guide bearing. Repairing the scored surface proved unacceptable and a new guide bearing needed to be installed.

Problems also began to appear on the finished surface of the dam. Surfacing cracks, not unusual on a job

as big as Shasta, needed to be cosmetically patched. Interestingly, cracks formed in rectangular areas ranging in size from a few inches to several feet on a side. The effected area usually represented the depth of a particular concrete pour and resulted from

Boaters on Lake Shasta could observe the final concrete placing.

premature curing. A special dry patch cement mix was applied and reapplied as necessary.

108

By May sufficient aggregate lie stored at the dam site and the process of shutting down and dismantling the world's longest conveyor belt proceeded. PCI found a South African firm, the Kimberly Diamond Mines, interested in purchasing the entire system, and it was sold to them for a one million dollar profit. Portions of the belt system were still in use decades later.

On through the summer months work moved ahead on installing electrical components in the powerhouse and switch-yard, stringing transmission lines, and placing concrete in the upper spillway blocks. Working in the searing July and August heat, men in bulldozers spent weeks backfilling the east and west abutments. Once backfilled road paving crews would come in and complete a permanent road connection to the top of the dam. The only major section left to complete was the three main drum gate foundation chambers. The work here needed to be precise in order to accommodate the precision engineered drum gates.

In October, the 102-foot spillway bridge beam arrived from the manufacturer on flat trailer-bed trucks. The huge steel cross girders were lifted by one of the main cableways cranes to temporary wooden piers on top of the dam. These mammoth monoliths would bear the full weight of the road bed above and supply enclosure for the drum gates. Men hurried about like ants checking the placement of the heavy beam; its resting place was unusual in that the support pier actually extended out over the dam, with the

The drum gates at the top of the spillway were installed late in the year.

counterbalancing pier located directly above the center line. Moving in cat-like fashion, sure-footed veterans ventured out onto the beam in order to disconnect the hoist lines. With four years of experience behind them, this kind of high-wire act seemed an everyday ordinary task.

November and December saw the last of the concrete placing and the completion of the switchyard. Most of the action centered on the drum gate roadbed and the two

The last bucket of concrete to the dam was placed on December 22, 1944.

elevator shaft-towers. Wanting to finish the concrete placing before Christmas, crews struggled in the last part of December to finish. As luck would have it, a powerful cloudburst dumped inches of rain on the dam site. Undaunted, foremen contrived a makeshift protective cover to shield the drying concrete; the men continued to work in the rain. Men waited patiently for breaks in the downpour to reset forms and call the headtower for another bucket of concrete. Then after quickly placing the load, another section of the canvas tent protective shield was hung over the newly placed section. This did not help those men attempting to pour their loads into forms on the two elevator towers. Work in this area slowed.

Finally, in a somewhat subdued formal ceremony conducted on December 22, 1944, the last bucket of concrete was placed. Actually, the concrete continued to be placed after the New Year; it took one additional day until

110

January 2, 1945 to complete the parapet walls of the elevator towers and to finish the Vista House (between the powerhouse and spillway). Everyone snapped pictures of the great event, knowing that for most of them, it would be their last big dam job. No other major dam construction projects were on the drawing boards, or even being talked about. Attention remained focused on America's all-out war effort.

PCI workers still on the payroll spent their time in early and mid-1945 dismantling the headtower, rounding-up and salvaging hundreds of tons of left over materials, and hauling off the entire conveyor belt system. A local real estate/construction company bought most of the small single family structures that had been home to PCI workers and trucked the houses down to Chico, a prosperous valley community. A few of the homes were set up in Redding. Some of these structures, being well built, remain in use today. Ironically, two of them were situated just down the hill from Frank Crowe's beautiful home in Redding. Dam workers in the boomtowns either moved to the Bay Area or some other Bureau job in the West. Still others entered military service expecting to see duty in the Pacific.

Homes in Shasta Dam Village, the contractor's camp, were sold and relocated in Chico and Redding.

With the word out that Shasta Dam had been completed, hundreds of visitors and some foreign government engineers came to see the mighty dam in operation. Tsin Yu Lin, Director of the Kunming Lakeside Electrical Works and Hui Huang, Director of the Bureau of Hydroelectric Survey were given a top priority tour of the entire dam site. They wanted to see every phase of the operation in hopes of using this information for several major dam projects planned on the Yellow River. Faced with their own water problems, Iranian engineers also

Visitors were greatly impressed to see finished Shasta Dam and the headtower.

visited at this time. Much of the worldwide recognition came from the dozens of foreign correspondents who visited. Mervyn Weston, Staff and War Correspondent of *The Argus* (Melbourne, Australia), smiled as he saw the breathtaking scene of Shasta Darn, Shasta Lake, and Mt. Shasta. Bureau of Reclamation visitors were constant. From Washington D. C. and regional offices came inspectors, managers, and curious engineers. Shasta Dam was big, and it was powerful, and everyone wanted to see it. In fact the crowds became so large and continuous that the Bureau converted an old International panel truck into a crowd control car, complete with loudspeakers. The Bureau tour guide moved along the dam roadway controlling crowd movement and giving impromptu lectures on dam construction and operation.

From 1946 until 1950 much finishing work went on at, and around the dam. One of the big jobs included installing the three gigantic drum gates and connecting the remaining three penstock tubes to the powerhouse. PCI employees left and were replaced by men hired directly by the Bureau. The upper and lower visitors' center needed interior work done. Bolting in the permanent guide rails running the full length of the dam crest roadway kept men at work for months. In and around the powerhouse crews finished last minute electrical and plumbing jobs.

The dedication of Shasta Dam, on June 17, 1950 signaled the formal governmental recognition of the completion of construction. Attending that day included: C. H. Purcell, State Director of Public Works; Richard L. Boke, Regional Bureau of Reclamation Director; Edwin Regan, State Senator; Congressman Clair Engle; and William E. Warne, Assistant Secretary of the Interior. Entertainment was provided by Hollywood star Danny Kaye, actor Leo Carrillo, and Metropolitan Opera star Florence Quartaro. After a series of speeches by visiting dignitaries, Assistant Secretary Warne threw the switch that opened the massive drum gates. Water, for the first time, raced out and down

The drum gates were opened during the official dedication of Shasta Dam in 1950.

113

the entire length of the 487-foot spill way, among sustained applause and gasps of excitement. Later, to cap off the ceremony, a dramatic evening light show, complete with fireworks enthralled spectators.

This photo is an aerial view of completed Shasta Dam.

Index

P

Pacific Constructors Inc., 10, 17, 19, 20-23, 25-26, 31-34, 38, 41, 43, 47-49, 51, 53, 57-58, 63, 65, 67-68, 74, 76, 80, 93, 102, 109, 111, 113
Page, John C., 29, 77
Parker Dam, 23-24, 41
Pearl Harbor, 79
penstocks, 50, 65, 72, 85, 87, 90, 97
Pit River Bridge, 25
Powerhouse, 108
Project City, 30

R

river diversion, 27, 31, 34, 36, 38, 41, 46, 53, 58, 76-77, 89, 95-98, 103-105
Rivers and Harbors Act, 18
Rumboltz, Matt, 33

S

Sacramento River, 8, 16, 19, 21, 26, 31-32, 36, 38, 41, 51, 53-54, 57, 59, 62-63, 70-72, 76-79, 86, 88-90, 95-96, 98, 103-105
safety at the dam site, 7, 42, 49, 53, 57, 67-68, 73-75, 78, 82
San Joaquin Valley, 15
scroll cases, 94
Shasta Dam Hospital, 69, 79

Shofner, Floyd, 20
Slocum, Harvey, 21
softball leagues, 50, 70
Southern Pacific railroad, 26, 31, 38
Summit City, 30

T

Thurston, D. W., 20
Town of Kennett, 26-30, 98, 103
Toyon, 29, 32-34, 43, 49-50, 66, 70, 80, 93, 102
Toyon School, 33
transmission lines, 19, 99, 106, 108-109

U

United States Bureau of Reclamation, 1-2, 8-9, 13, 19-20, 23, 25-26, 28-29, 32, 34, 38, 42, 47, 50, 56, 64, 67-68, 70, 74, 77, 79, 86, 89, 94, 98, 102-103, 107-108, 111-113

W

Whinnery, Ray, 21
Wood, Clyde, 20, 48
working at night, 65
World War II, 6, 9, 102

Y

Young, Walker, 29, 56

CPSIA information can be obtained
at www.ICGtesting.com
Printed in the USA
LVHW101003210819
628437LV00004B/80/P